IN THE COUNTRY OF HEARTS

IN THE COUNTRY OF HEARTS

Journeys in the Art of Medicine

JOHN STONE

Delacorte Press

Published by
Delacorte Press
Bantam Doubleday Dell Publishing Group, Inc.
666 Fifth Avenue
New York, New York 10103

Library of Congress Cataloging in Publication Data

Stone, John, 1936–
    In the country of hearts : journeys in the art of medicine / John Stone.
        p.   cm.
    ISBN 0-385-30169-3
    1. Cardiology—Miscellanea.   I. Title.
    RC669.S816   1990
    616.1'2—dc20   90-31474
                                                                    CIP

Manufactured in the United States of America
Published simultaneously in Canada

September 1990

10   9   8   7   6   5   4   3   2   1

RRD

for Lu, for Johnny, for Jim
three necessary hearts

Acknowledgments

Many people helped in the preparation of this book. My debt to Mae Nelson is a continuing one: she has assisted with each of my earlier books. She knows my voice and, sometimes before I do, what I am hoping to say. Her optimism, her attention to detail, and her invaluable suggestions are greatly appreciated.

To Mel Konner I am also especially grateful: for his example within the world of writing, for his sage advice at various junctures, and, most importantly, for his friendship.

I have had the good fortune to work with four people whom I have come to think of as blessings in the disguise of editors. The first of these must be Holcomb Noble of *The New York Times Magazine*. I hope he already knows my gratitude for his editorial skill, his sensitivity to the language, and for his friendship. Patricia Gadsby of *Discover* has encouraged me during the writing of several of these pieces. Jane Rosenman was the first editor to write me with the notion that a book might be in the offing; I will always be grateful for her enthusiastic and deeply literate shepherding of my work. Bob Miller, editorial director of Delacorte Press, has provided expert editorial guidance, a sustaining sense of humor, and an extraordinary willingness to have the author participate in the many decisions that must be made in the course of production.

For their close reading of many of these pieces, their insightful comments, and for their friendship, I am indebted to Sally Wolff and to Frances Hevenor. Special thanks, too, to many of my medical colleagues for their expert advice. Sophronia Allen and Harry Foster and the staff of the Cardiac Clinic of the Georgia Children's Medical Service have been unfailingly helpful. My agent, Elaine Markson, has provided encouragement and expertise during my journey through the world of publishing.

Finally, it is a special pleasure to acknowledge my deep gratitude to those who have taught me at every turn: students, colleagues, and, most especially, patients.

—John Stone

Contents

IN THE COUNTRY OF HEARTS

Introduction

$\mathcal{E}$ach of us is born with two hearts. One is the literal heart, the fist-sized pumping one that looms like a ghost on the chest X ray. The other heart is a metaphorical one, one that pumps no blood at all. More about the metaphorical heart presently, except to say that I encountered it early on—everyone does—long before I studied cardiology.

The literal heart is, of course, a pump, commissioned to its Sisyphian labor in the embryo, where its beat begins as a microscopic nudge, then a ripple. Thereafter, the heart is obliged, by only partly understood laws, to sing for its lifelong supper. Onerous duty it may be, but the heart seems to revel in it, thumping tirelessly, one of the happy things that go bump in the night. Its work places each of us in its debt, though it's easy not to think about the heart unless trouble arises.

But the heart is not simply a mechanical pump of pressure heads, resistances, ergs and dynes, like the one that pumps water fitfully to the top of my mountain at Cherry Log, Georgia. No—though it *is* all that and more. For one thing, the heart is more dependable than the pump at

Cherry Log: it provides three billion heartbeats for the average person in a lifetime—and even that huge number, as we live longer, continues to spiral upward in a kind of benevolent cardiac inflation. All of this cardiac work is bequeathed to us as human beings, with no down-time, no lubrication, no oil changes required. Moreover, the heart as a pump is more interesting than the one that provides my shower at Cherry Log. The heart, after all, is not merely a contraption of steel, pistons, and gauges, but is an intricate universe of muscle and valves, arteries and veins, plus a sophisticated electrical system that surpasses the circuitry of the *Voyager* spaceship, if only in terms of durability and steadfastness.

One of the reasons I chose cardiology as a career is that way back, before medical school, cardiology seemed instinctively to make sense to me—sense in ways that endocrinology or nephrology or gastroenterology did not. Moreover (though I denied it was a factor at the time), I had a strong personal motivation to study the heart: My own father died of a heart attack when he was only forty-five-years old. I was then a senior in high school. Years later, at my request, the physician who cared for my father showed me his last EKG, the one taken just before his death. By then I knew what to look for, the squiggles of that EKG pointing clearly to the culprit clot in the coronary artery. Trying to do something about such a senseless and premature loss seemed a good way to spend a life. Certainly I could think of no better at the time; even now, I'd be hard-pressed to do so.

It may be that medicine was in my genes, though my father was not a physician. After college, during the Depression, he rose from a first job as packer on the conveyor line to become production supervisor for a large glass bottle company, Knox Glass. He would have made a good physician, though. Once, at the glass factory, a fellow worker was injured in an accident; his neck had been slashed and he was bleeding heavily. My father knelt by the injured man there amid the machinery roar, next to the hellfire of the huge furnace (with its lava of molten glass), and coolly applied pressure over the man's neck, stopping the bleeding until help arrived. My father had, in abundance, one of the most important prerequisites for medicine: He liked people. So did his father (my grandfather), who was a general practitioner in northeast Mississippi for more than fifty years. His practice included house calls with horse and buggy; his usual fees ranged from barter to fifty cents to two dollars. He was an inveterate and humorous storyteller (and letter writer). I remember well his doctor's bag full of mysteries, and the wondrous antiseptic smell that swept with him into the room. In his office (across the road from his house), on one shelf, he kept, preserved in a bottle, the body of a small stillborn child; once, in a poem, I wondered, "What magic did he use it for?" I wish I knew his answer. Finally, one of my father's brothers has been a busy family practitioner for decades in a town in Mississippi not far from where all the Stones grew up. When I was in my teens, and an avid reader, people often remarked to me that Uncle Orville had also liked to read when he was my age; some even wondered aloud whether I, too, was considering medicine. I was, I was.

In the decades since my father's death, there has been a revolution in cardiac care. Increasingly, medicine is able to *do* something about heart disease. The milestones include the heart–lung machine; artificial heart valves and pacemakers; the defibrillator (which, had it been available, might well have reversed my father's terminal cardiac rhythm); cardiac transplantation; balloon angioplasty and bypass grafts for the coronary arteries; a whirlwind of new drugs and diagnostic tools. Still, heart disease continues as the leading cause of death in the United States. The treatment of patients with heart disease, therefore, remains humbling. That fact will be clear as the various advances in cardiology take on human shapes, triumphant and sobering, within this book.

Virgil, in *The Aeneid*, observed, "Here are the tears of things; mortality touches the heart." For a cardiologist, that is close to the truth of the matter. Though each of us lives with death *potentially* just around the corner (a random accident on a busy expressway, for example), most of us manage to repress the idea of our own mortality for months or years at a time. For the cardiologist (and the poet), this is not possible: he feels the weight of mortality daily, not only in his bones, but in their marrow. This awareness comes, in part, because cardiac death may occur so suddenly, in a cataclysm, like a "terrible, swift sword." For the heart, symbol of life, is also the final common pathway along which death must stride. I addressed this subject once in a poem:

> Death
>
> I have seen   come on
> slowly as rust
> sand
>
> or suddenly   as when
> someone leaving
> a room
>
> finds the doorknob
> come loose in his hand

That sensation of finality, of helplessness, the feeling of the cool doorknob against the living palm is something cardiologists must learn to expect—and work to forestall. Our job, often enough, is to try to make come true—at least for a while—John Donne's hope (or prediction): "Death, thou shalt die!"

An allied part of the cardiologist's job, though, is to know when to *stop* trying. It is this part of the job (which all physicians and all patients share) that requires the greatest skill, in a sense. For once one has learned *what* to do and *how* to do it, the main question is *whether* to do it—we must learn to better gauge, for any given intervention, what the human return is likely to be; to recognize that moment when the technology available, dazzling as it is, is simply not enough, when the pain of maintaining life is worse than the pain of letting go.

More than 350 years ago, the English physician William Harvey labored to make sense of the circulation. Of his work, he wrote, "I found the task so truly arduous, so full of difficulties, that I was almost tempted to think . . . that the motion of the heart was only to be comprehended by God." But Harvey persevered. In his master work, *De Motu Cordis,* he described his observations and explained the circle of the circulation for us all. Other scientists had nibbled away at the mysteries of the circulation, but it was William Harvey who "convinced the world," as William Osler phrased it. All physicians today, to some degree, are indebted to William Harvey for his translation of what he'd seen during his long sojourn in the country of hearts. And all physicians must aspire to the excellence of Harvey's translation. For *translation,* "a carrying across," is one activity that is sorely needed in medicine today. Communication between human beings is, and has always been, difficult; but the language of medicine, increasingly arcane and technologically based, must be translated into the common language of us all. We must try to speak together.

To this point, I have only mentioned that fraternal twin of the literal heart, the metaphorical heart. I am speaking now of the heart as a synonym for sensibility, sensitivity, as the seat of the emotions, if you will—the heart about which Pascal wrote, "The heart has its reasons which reason knows nothing of." *That* heart. All fully rational people presume that our emotions spring from the electrical and biochemical corridors of the *brain*; but for many writers (incorrigible as they are) and cardiologists, this proposition is difficult to accept. Was it not William Faulkner who said that the writer must leave "no room in his workshop for anything but the old verities and truths of the heart . . .

love and honor and pity and pride and compassion and sacrifice"? Hence, the metaphorical heart.

If, as Carson McCullers surmised, "the heart is a lonely hunter," it is also a wondrous storyteller. Physicians, among others, are privileged to hear these compelling tales. It is a kind of short story, after all, that brings a person to the physician in the first place; then, over time, the chapters of that person's life shape themselves into as idiosyncratic a novel as ever was written. Within that novel, the physician can become an important character as he helps his patients cope with their hearts through illnesses short and long, through childbirth and infections, through cardiac surgery, as they triumph and as they falter. I feel fortunate to have played a role in some of these human stories, despite the setbacks that come, inevitably, with living and working in the various universes of the heart.

The heart, then, is infinitely more than a powerful engine, a perpetual-motion machine, a mail carrier on its appointed rounds. The literal heart is at the very center of our lives: without it, we would all be dead. But the metaphorical heart tempers the literal one and adds an extra dimension. Without a metaphorical heart, we'd all be in the position of the Tin Man in *The Wizard of Oz*. The cutout heart that so thrilled the Tin Man is precisely what we would all miss tomorrow morning if we woke up without our metaphorical pumps. And that might be worse than being dead.

Recently I came across two photographs that were taken while I was in medical school. One, in anatomy lab, catches me standing by the side of an articulated skeleton; both of us are smiling broadly while I study the bones of his forearm. The second photo, two years later, shows me bent over the bed of a patient, listening intently to his heart. (Aural memory is wondrous: to this day, I can remember clearly that man's labored and abnormal heart sounds.) The young man in that second photo was already intensely interested in matters cardiac. In the decades since that photograph, that young man has shed his short white coat for a long one; he has put on a few pounds and years, grown a beard. Nevertheless, this book was written out of that young man's abiding fascination with the motions of the heart. It reflects twenty-five years of immersion in the human encounter that is medicine.

Emily Dickinson, in one of her best poems, notes,

> "The Soul selects her own Society —
> Then—shuts the Door—."

It seems to me now, looking back, that cardiology selected me at least as much as I selected it. I feel fortunate, all these years, to have been a member of the society of hearts. Thus, for my part, I'd emend Dickinson's line to have it read:

> "The *Heart* selects its own Society . . ."

But I'd add that for all those who are interested in the heart—literal, metaphorical, or both—the door is always open.

PART ONE
Languages of
the Heart

◈

Blue Baby

◈

Many nursery rhymes are hard to fathom, especially for adults, which raises the question of why we teach them to our children. Even if we don't teach them, our children know them, as though these singsong rhythms had been transmitted across the placenta during intrauterine life. The prime prerequisites of such poems is that they move gracefully and please the ear of a child. As we grow up we leave the characters of most nursery rhymes to languish inside their sometimes cautionary, often nonsensical tales: Little Jack Horner, Georgie Porgie, Little Miss Muffet. But as for Little Boy Blue, there is a very real story about him.

$\mathcal{J}$f we are to begin at the beginning, it must be way back. In the yolk of time. The problem began with the embryo, the cells of which divide, burgeon, twist, and unfold, yielding to the wash of DNA and the codes of its helix. The embryo is an architect; it must invent, out of all that has gone before, the city it plans to inhabit. The work is precise and delicate; the wonder is that trouble doesn't occur more often. Virtually all creatures develop in this way: that is why the premedical student can study the stages of growth of the chick embryo and extrapolate to the human. Thus, every human embryo, passing through the gill-slit stage on its way to lungs, rehearses the moves of the chicken that has crossed this road so many times before, effortlessly, within the chalk walls of the mother shell. It is a magical act, predestination come to pass, a virtuoso performance until, in this case, somewhere between the fifth and seventh weeks of pregnancy, when it came inexplicably to grief: a million commandments all obeyed to the letter, except for the one that matters to Jeremy.

Jeremy is almost two years old; he first came to the clinic because a heart murmur was heard shortly after birth. Though small for his age, he is alert and bright. Jeremy's condition is called tetralogy of Fallot (Fah-*low*), the most common cause of the so-called blue baby. Study of his cardiac anatomy with the echocardiograph has been diagnostic for tetralogy: the sonar waves outlined two main and interconnected problems: narrowing and partial obstruction of the artery to the lungs; and a defect, a hole, in the wall, or septum, that divides the right and left ventricles, a ventricular septal defect. Though the French physician Etienne Fallot, in 1888, described *four* problems (hence, *tetra*logy), these two basic defects account for Jeremy's blueness. Dark unoxygenated blood surges through the veins back to the heart from the body (where it has given up its oxygen); entering the right ventricle, this venous blood finds the way to the lungs partially blocked, so takes the path of less resistance, across the septal defect into the left ventricle. There, the dark "blue" blood mixes with the bright red oxygenated blood headed out to the body: that is why Jeremy's skin is blue, why his growth has been slow. Most alarming today, his blueness is worse.

Jeremy, says his mother, has been more listless since his last clinic visit three months ago: not eating as well, resting more, playing less. "And his lips and fingers turn real dark blue after he plays hard," she says. I let Jeremy sit on his mother's lap and ease my stethoscope under his shirt. He doesn't cry; he's a veteran at this. The loud murmur is unchanged. But his mother is right, as mothers often are: Jeremy *is* bluer today; his nail beds, his lips, are not simply bluish, they're purple. As Jeremy falls quietly to sleep on his mother's lap, I seize the opportunity to take a quick reading on the oximeter, which gauges, painlessly, the oxygenation of the blood.

The pulse oximeter is a recent technology that uses light sensors to measure the ratio of unoxygenated to oxygenated blood passing through the vessels of the finger or ear. The instrument monitors, continuously, for "blueness," or cyanosis. The widest use of oximetry is in the detection of possibly lethal falls in the blood oxygen of patients in operating rooms and intensive care units (where it has already prevented hundreds of deaths).

The nurse slips Jeremy's index finger into the padded chamber; within seconds, there's a readout of the arterial blood oxygen saturation: 73 percent. I stick my own finger in, the gadget beeps: 94 percent. The obstruction in the artery to Jeremy's lungs is gradually worsening. He will definitely need surgery—and soon. I explain this to the mother, still holding Jeremy, asleep like a dusky statue in her arms. She doesn't cry either. She's been expecting this.

More than twenty-five years ago, I flew from Georgia to the Mayo Clinic in the hold of a huge military transport plane, one volunteered by the local air force base. A nurse, Alice, flew with me as we ferried a cyanotic infant, only a few weeks old, who also had tetralogy of Fallot. The child, William, was more seriously ill than Jeremy—much smaller, bluer. Alice and I had rigged up, in the vaulted whale's belly of the plane, a bassinette that swung lightly, like a cradle, from the arching ribs of the hull. The plane was too noisy for much talk, but we could see what was happening. William was fine, only slightly blue, as long as he slept. But when he began to cry, his marginal circulation deteriorated: he then got bluer and bluer, until, at times, he actually lost consciousness transiently because of lack of oxygen. Oxygen was being piped into his bassinette, but when he cried, either Alice or I picked him up quickly and shushed him. Twice during our trip, it was necessary to give William a small shot of morphine: the drug worked within a few seconds to calm him and put him gently back to sleep, while his color changed, by slow degrees, from blue back toward pink in a kind of living litmus test. Both Alice and I were grateful when the plane touched down at dusk on the snowy Minnesota runway and we could turn our passenger over to the staff at Mayo. Within twenty-four hours, William had had his surgery, a palliative procedure that would allow him a chance to grow, in the hope of definitive surgery later. When I last saw him, before he moved to a neighboring state, he was five years old, pink, sassy, and growing.

Until 1944, no surgery for tetralogy was available. Then, at Johns Hopkins, Helen Taussig, a pediatrician, and

Alfred Blalock, a surgeon, devised an ingenious approach. They decided to "bypass" the narrowed pulmonary artery, suturing a (dispensable) arm artery to the pulmonary artery just past the obstruction. Drs. Blalock and Taussig were gratified that their patients "pinked up" immediately. For years, the Blalock–Taussig shunt (or variants) was the only help available for tetralogy; though this surgery was palliative, its results were dramatic, even miraculous, when one considers that, for centuries, parents and physicians had stood helplessly by while "blue babies" worsened and eventually died. Complete surgical correction of tetralogy required that the heart itself, sacrosanct and inviolate, be opened; this step had to await development of the "heart–lung machine," the kind to be used in Jeremy's care.

As surgeons prepare to place Jeremy on a heart–lung machine now greatly refined from the first models so as to accommodate infants, his heart—the size and color of a large plum—beats within his opened chest. First, all the blood coming back to Jeremy's heart through the veins is diverted through tubing to the machine, which oxygenates, removes carbon dioxide, filters, cools or heats, and pumps the blood coming to it. (Heart–lung machines are of several types, but basically they use either a bubble oxygenator or a semi-permeable membrane that mimics the functions of the lung. The blood, thus oxygenated, is cooled or heated, as necessary, then pumped back into the patient's aorta and out to the body, simulating the function of the heart.)

The pump technician announces, "We're on bypass."

The child's body is cooled, a step that decreases metabolism and protects the brain, kidneys, and other vital organs. As the temperature falls his heart slows, then, no longer needed, is allowed to stop.

Each member of the surgical team is intent as the surgeons work through the small, brightly lit operative field. All this technology, art and science, in the service of one small plum—which is now ready to be opened by the surgeon.

Jeremy's ventricular septal defect is large, the size of a dime. It is closed by a patch made of Dacron, carefully sewn at the margins into the surrounding heart muscle. The pulmonary artery is opened and widened, using a patch made of Jeremy's own pericardium (the tough sac that encloses the heart). All the while, the drone of the pump is heard, taking in Jeremy's dark blood through one tube and pumping it back, bright red, to his body through another. His heart is now being sewn closed. The little patient has been on bypass just over an hour; we are ready to wean him from the machine.

Jeremy's temperature is raised—and, spontaneously, his heart begins to beat again.

The strength of the heartbeat increases gradually, taking over more and more of the pumping function. He's off bypass now, on his own, and flying. The surgeon's eyes smile and I know his mouth is smiling too. The anesthesiologist doesn't really need to look at the oximeter reading, only at Jeremy's lips. He looks anyway.

Now, as I see Jeremy in the clinic three weeks later, he's certainly not listless; he toys with the blood pressure cuff, tries to explore the garbage can. The midline incision in his breastbone is healing nicely. He seems not to notice it at all, his mother says. He's eating well, breathing easily. His arterial saturation is the same as mine: 94 percent. With any luck, he should be cured. He should be ready for kindergarten when it comes, able to keep up with the other kids. His mother smiles gently down at her son, three weeks into his second childhood. Jeremy's lips are pink. On this afternoon, that is the only thing in this world that matters.

Telltale Hands

In its most felicitous form, the practice of cardiology maintains its roots in internal medicine, from which it sprang. As the great physician William Osler reminds us, "The chief function of the consultant is to make a rectal examination that you have omitted." The cardiologist's true realm, therefore, is not just the heart, but the entire body. When a patient is seen for the first time, it's crucial that a thorough physical examination be done. Worthy of special attention are the hands, which may offer clues not only to heart disease but to disease in other organs (the thyroid, for example) that may secondarily affect the heart. García Lorca wrote, "The poet is a professor of the five bodily senses." So, in the happiest of circumstances, is the cardiologist.

She's here because of her yellow hands. As she holds them out for me to examine, I'm reminded for a moment of the way in which women, under old Moslem custom, were examined by the physician: only the hands, thrust demurely through a curtain, were allowed to be scrutinized. My patient's hands are beautiful, like an advertisement for hand lotion. But they *are* yellow, especially the palms. I take a history, ruling out liver disease by looking at the whites of her eyes (where jaundice makes its appearance). Then, as recommended by Willie Sutton, the bank robber, I go "where the money is": I ask about her diet. The answer spills out: She's been on an austere regimen, one in which, she was told, she could eat as many raw vegetables as she wished. Her favorite snack, for months, has been carrots. And that's the answer: She's eaten so many carrots that she's accumulated high blood levels of beta-carotene, a yellow pigment with a special affinity for the skin of the hands and feet. I ask to see her feet: the soles are bright yellow. I reassure her that, over the next few months, the pigmentation will gradually disappear. Once again, the hands have told their story, as eloquently as any tongue.

For a while after World War II, when a kid went to buy a new pair of shoes, the fit was sometimes checked with a fluoroscope (until someone sounded the alarm about X rays). I remember standing up on the machine and plugging in my feet; there was a humming noise, then I would see my bones wiggling like chalk inside the leather. That was my first peek at interior anatomy and it proved the old spiritual true: the toebone *is* connected to the footbone. I reasoned that the wristbone must therefore be connected to the handbone and the fingerbones. Thirteen years later, in anatomy class, it was the hand, complex in form, wondrous in function, that fascinated me most.

The most inept anatomy student finds twenty-seven bones in the hand, including the eight in the wrist. Next are five metacarpals, the ends of which form the knuckles. And finally, the small bones of the fingers, the phalanges, fourteen in all (three for each of the fingers, only two for the thumb). The bones are joined by ligaments and separated by small joint spaces. But we need not dissect any further; let's just study the terrain.

Rendering the hand in paint or marble has tantalized artists for centuries. The *handscape* is a subtle one, with meandering superficial veins on the back—these vessels, engorged when the hand is held downward, collapse as the hand is raised and blood streams back into the heart. As the hand clenches, then opens, tendons can be seen at play under the skin. As for the muscles of the hand, here, too, much can be deduced from observation. As you make a tight fist, then relax it, watch, then feel, the muscles in your upper forearm. The bulging there confirms an important anatomical fact: the forearm muscles, the extrinsic muscles of the hand, manipulate the fingers from a distance, like marionettes. Each muscle is attached to the fingers by long white tendons that course from the forearm over the wrist, and out to the fingers. The intrinsic muscles, those within the hand proper, work to fan the fingers apart and bring them back together; they also allow the thumb to oppose (to touch) each of the fingers, an important human feature that lower primates lack.

It's been estimated that the human hand makes a thousand different movements during a single day, ranging from the intricate to the coarse. The fingers and thumb bend like hinges; each can also rotate, a movement that increases their utility. The royalty of rotation, though, is the wrist, evidenced by its etymology (from Old English, *wraestan*, to twist or wrest). The idea for the universal joint in a car's power train (according to a friend who understands such things) was conceived while the inventor watched the twirling of his wife's wrists.

When I see a new patient, I find it valuable, at that first meeting, *consciously* to look at the hands. Clues to diseases in the nervous system, heart, lung, liver, and other organs can be found there. My mental notes begin with the handshake: temperature, moisture, texture, color, strength. Take temperature, for example: An overactive thyroid gland results in a warm, moist hand. A cool hand is seen in patients with Raynaud's phenomenon (due to arterial spasm, which also results in color changes, and occurs most often in collagen vascular diseases, such as lupus). Calluses, scars, and stains on the hands may reflect the patient's occupational status. Sherlock Holmes could tell at a glance the "handedness" of a laborer: the dominant hand is often slightly larger and more muscular than the nondominant one. Arthritis, especially the rheumatoid variety, often makes its appearance in the hand joints. Pallor of the palmar creases suggests anemia. A "pill-rolling" tremor may be linked with a patient's masklike face and shuffling gait to confirm Parkinsonism. Liver spots, usually flat brown discolorations on the back of the hand, are pigmentary changes caused by aging and sun exposure, and are unrelated to the liver. But redness of the palms, especially the heels of the palms, *can* suggest liver disease.

The nails are cousins to hoof and horn; useful for offense or defense, they range from the daggerlike, outfitted with glitter, to the merely bitten. In medicine, they can also be unique evidence of *past* disease. The nails of someone who had pneumonia several weeks previously may now show transverse grooves—these "Beau's lines" attest mutely to the nutritional insult to the nail plate (the growing part of the nail, under the cuticle). Similar lines may appear in the nails of the intended victim of slow murder with arsenic. (Detectives assigned to such cases must be mindful lest their evidence disappear: a normal nail completely replaces itself in three to six months.) A broad short thumb (and nail) with a blunted tip, a "murderer's thumb," is often a familial trait that has nothing to do with homicide. But "clubbing" of the nails, a bulbous enlargement of the fingertips, is often diagnostic of certain lung diseases and congenital heart problems. Such clues may well suggest which laboratory tests will be useful to the physician.

Fingers, like people, may be long or short, but there can be pathological aspects of finger length. The celebrated violinist Niccolò Paganini had extremely long fingers. He may also have had Marfan's syndrome. Long, spidery digits (arachnodactyly) and an abnormally tall body structure may suggest this syndrome, a disorder of connective tissue that affects many organs, notably the heart and aorta. Sudden death in a basketball player (because of rupture of the aorta) may be due to unsuspected Marfan's. It's also been suggested that Abraham Lincoln's lanky stature and long, narrow face were the result of this process.

The number of digits isn't always five: both polydactyly (more than five digits) and syndactyly (fusion of the fingers) occur with some frequency. Either may signal the simultaneous presence of congenital heart disease. (Development of the heart and the hand in the embryo occur at about the same time. The triggers for such defects—and most of the time we don't know the cause—are thus likely to affect both structures.)

Dermatoglyphics (*derma*, "skin," plus *glyphic*, "carvings") is the fancy name for the study of lines and whorls in the palms, soles, and digits. Not only physicians study these: on the palm, there are lines (heart, life, fate, head) by which the fortune-teller comes to mystical assertions. Medically, the most recognizable palmar line is the so-called simian crease, a single transverse furrow that extends across the whole palm and is found in perhaps 50 percent of patients with Down syndrome (who commonly have broad, short hands with a short, incurving little finger). Most normal palms have three or four major overlapping lines that extend partway across the palm—but I always tell medical students (most of whom are hypochondriacs at some point) that some *normal* people have a single palmar line similar to the simian one.

One of my aunts has been deaf since childhood; my mother, a hearing person, taught for decades in a state school for the deaf. I'd be remiss, then, not to mention the most obvious language of the hands, sign language. One mark of enlightenment in our time (though still too limited) is the presence, on television, of captioned programming or an occasional translator signing for the deaf audience.

In medicine, a hand is never merely a hand; symbolically, it is much more. That is why the "laying on of hands" is so important for physician and patient. A cancer surgeon I know always holds his patient's hand when he visits—he tells me that, in this way, a *short* visit to the bedside is perceived by the patient as being longer than it really is. In any event, such hand-to-hand contact is a better effort toward healing than mumbling distractedly while flipping through a burgeoning chart.

Hands figure importantly in virtually every human action and reaction: love, grief, prayer, rage, seduction, and farewell. The American writer (and misanthrope) Ambrose Bierce, in his *Devil's Dictionary*, defines *hand* as a "singular instrument worn at the end of the human arm and commonly thrust into somebody's pocket." Ah, but Ambrose, you miss the point. What grace and deftness there is in even the meanest motions of the hands, whatever work they are about.

◈

The Long House
Call

◈

Like most everyone, I remember house calls now through a haze of
fever, through the fogged-up windows of time. It was Dr. Felder who
swept into my room and perched on my bed when I was a youngster
and sick. He smelled like *hospital*; his stethoscope was so cold, it
burned. He *always* looked at my throat: he would ask me to pant like
a dog, then pry my mouth open with a wooden tongue depressor until
I gagged. Dr. Felder's house calls often culminated in an injection of
one of the new antibiotics he carried in his black bag. The drugs had
fancy names ending in *mycin*—the most glittering example sprang from
the Latin root *aureus*, meaning "golden": Aureomycin. But, as I was to
learn on my own, there are benefits of house calls—on both sides—
that far outlast the temporary soreness in one's rump.

$\mathcal{T}$he day comes, by and by, when Chicken Little's prediction seems to be coming true: The sky *is* falling. It was at about that time in her life that I first met Mrs. Corrigan.

She was sixty years old and I was thirty-two, in my second year of cardiology training. A small woman, she stood less than five feet tall, with gray hair pulled back tightly into a bun, but her most constant feature was a smile; it shone through even her worry when she saw me for the first time in the cardiac clinic. She had come to the clinic with two main symptoms. First, she had chest pain whenever she walked too fast—present for six months or so, the pain would ease off when she rested but now came more frequently and lasted longer. Second, and more worrisome to her—and to me—she'd begun to get very dizzy, light-headed, with exercise. Twice, carrying a sack of groceries from the store back up the hill to her house, she'd not only had chest pain but had almost fainted, too. When I examined her on that first visit, the cause of her symptoms was immediately clear.

Her blood pressure was on the low side. I felt her pulse in the carotid artery in her neck; it was weak, difficult to detect. Unlike the usual thumping carotid artery, her pulse rose only reluctantly to the examining finger. At the base of her neck, on the chest wall, there was an easily felt shudder, a rough vibration with each pulse, like a cat's purr. When I listened to her heart, rather than the expected crisp "lup-dup," I heard a gruff, harsh sound like the clearing of a throat, a murmur so loud that it could be heard even with the stethoscope an eighth of an inch or so *off* the chest wall. It was no great Oslerian feat of diagnosis on my part to suspect that she had severe *aortic stenosis*.

I explained to her that she had a diseased valve in her heart. Her aortic valve, through which blood exits from the left ventricle (the heart's main pumping chamber) into the aorta (the body's main artery) was severely narrowed. Hence her chest pain, thus her dizziness: when exercise put greater demands on her heart, it could not supply sufficient blood and oxygen either to her brain or to the heart itself. When I told her a cardiac catheterization would be necessary to measure just how bad the narrowing was, she nodded in agreement. Mrs. Corrigan knew something had to be done. For my part, I knew it had to be done quickly: sudden unexpected death, often during exercise, may occur in some patients with severe aortic stenosis. Such deaths may be heralded by chest pain or dizziness, such as she'd had.

At that time, in the late 1960s, I was still learning how to do cardiac caths: I hadn't done that many. In performing a cath, a tube, or catheter, is guided, under fluoroscopy, from the femoral artery (at the top of the leg) backward against the flow in the aorta. In Mrs. Corrigan's case, I wanted to measure the pressures on either side of her valve, both in the aorta and in the left ventricle. I suspected, though, that her valve might be so narrowed, it might be difficult to pass the catheter across it. I was right.

A few days later, in the darkened cath lab, she and I both worked up a sweat, but the catheter just would *not* slip down into the ventricle. I tried until both she and I were exhausted. We very much needed to measure the pressure in the ventricle: elevation of the pressure there, "upstream" from the narrowed valve, was an all-important index of the severity of the narrowing.

These days, we could use an ultrasound examination of the heart—a Doppler echocardiogram—to give us an indirect and noninvasive measure of her aortic stenosis. We might even use the exquisite eye of magnetic resonance imaging (MRI) to picture the diseased valve. But neither option was available at the time. In short, diagnosis would be easier now; then, it was difficult. I talked to the cardiac surgeon and we agreed there was only one approach left to us—a direct needle puncture of the heart, the left ventricle, through the chest wall, under local anesthesia.

The day of that puncture is indelible in my mind. Mrs. Corrigan was in good spirits, lying on the table in the cath lab while her chest was cleaned with antiseptics and the local anesthetic was introduced into the skin through a small needle. The surgeon was to perform the ventricular puncture. In case there was trouble, such as a laceration of the heart, with bleeding that could be fatal, the operating room was on "standby" so that surgery to control the bleeding could be done immediately. Fortunately, the needle entered the heart easily. And it told us what we needed to know—the blood that spurted from the ventricle was under tremendous pressure, making the diagnosis certain. I still remember the needle in her chest twitching rhythmically as the heart wriggled like a speared fish on the other end. Mrs. Corrigan didn't bat an eye. Three days later, she had surgery to replace her diseased valve with an artificial one.

From the top, the aortic side, the normal aortic valve looks a bit like a pie that's been divided into thirds. Hinged at the periphery and closing tightly at the center of the circle, the three wedge-shaped sections of the valve are made of thin white, extraordinarily tough tissue that can withstand the three billion openings and closings it must make in a lifetime. But Mrs. Corrigan's valve, we suspected, was rigid, ringed about with stalagmites of calcium that jutted into the geyser of blood as it left the ventricle, creating enough turbulence to cause both the heart murmur and the "cat's purr" I'd found when I examined her.

Nowadays, Mrs. Corrigan would have been a candidate for a porcine (pig) heart valve, which so closely resembles the human one. But the valve we had then—and still often use today because it's so reliable—looked nothing like the gracile aortic valve we are born with. The valve Mrs. Corrigan was to receive was the latest model of the Starr–Edwards valve, an ingenious device first created in the 1950s. To me, it looks most like a tiny birdcage with a Ping-Pong ball inside it. Contraction of the heart forces the Ping-Pong ball upward, allowing blood to surge into the aorta (movement of the ball is restrained by the cage); when the heart relaxes, the ball drops down and seals off any leak of blood back into the heart.

During the surgery, Mrs. Corrigan was first placed on the heart–lung machine, which took over the job of circulating blood and oxygen to her brain and other vital organs. The machine made it possible to stop her own heart completely, so that the surgeon's delicate work could proceed. When he removed the diseased valve, it looked as bad as we'd thought it would, its narrow pinpoint opening encrusted with spicules of calcium, hard as bone. (No wonder I hadn't been able to get the catheter through it!) Then the artificial valve was sutured into place. And the operating team began to wean her from the pump. I remember heaving a sigh of relief as the valve began its "click-click, click-click" there in the cool, tiled hissing operating room. I felt her carotid pulse. It was bounding and healthy, even as she slept on, oblivious.

Three weeks after her surgery, Mrs. Corrigan called me up on a Saturday to ask if I'd like to come to her house in south Atlanta and pick figs. I said *yes* immediately. Thus began a long series of house calls.

Her house was only a few miles from the hospital; I found it easily that morning, driving up the steep hill that used to defeat her when she walked. She'd already picked the figs—and some vegetables, too—from the bountiful garden behind her old house. She and I sat for a long while on her back steps, chatting. She looked good. In the quiet of her backyard, from time to time, I could hear the faint clicking of her aortic valve. Then she offered to give me a tour of her house. So this, I thought as we walked around, is where the aortic stenosis used to live.

I met her son-in-law, greeted her husband. She showed me her bedroom and the multiple pill bottles, heart medicines, on the bedside table. Two objects on that guided tour stand out in my memory; both were in her bedroom. On the wall there was a lighted portrait of Christ that was transformed into an image of the Virgin Mary when one viewed it from different angles. And on the chest of drawers, there was a music box the likes of which I had never seen. Above the box twirled an empty whiskey decanter in the shape of a nineteenth-century British soldier. As the red-caped soldier rotated, the music box played "How Dry I Am."

She told me she was doing well—no chest pain; no dizziness. That was a gift, she said, that I had given her. I staggered to my car under the weight of *her* gifts to me: the figs, the vegetables, her gratitude.

I followed Mrs. Corrigan closely for years. Usually, when she came to the cardiac clinic and found she was scheduled to see a doctor other than me, she would make her way to my office and there, in the relative quiet, away from the bustle of the clinic, insist that I listen to her heart. I would always say that it was as regular as a clock and she would always smile.

On the day of my original house call, I began writing a poem about Mrs. Corrigan. In the poem, I contrasted a normal heart valve with her artificial one, deciding, "I know how clumsy it is." Yet her new valve worked beautifully and steadily. In the writing of that poem, I discovered a personal definition of health: "Health is whatever works/and for as long." That is a definition I can still defend to this day.

Some months after the publication of the volume containing my poem about her, Mrs. Corrigan came to my office with a copy of the book, holding it out to me and smiling, "That's *me* in the poem, isn't it?"

"It sure is," I replied, and signed her copy with deep pleasure.

Mrs. Corrigan continued to do well. She did have to take anticoagulants daily—blood thinners—to prevent clots from forming on the surfaces of the valve. But she escaped any serious bleeding episodes that might have occurred. And she remained active, taking care of her family, continuing to garden. Often, in the summer, she made a "reverse house call" to the hospital, bringing to my office large sacks of vegetables for me and my secretary.

But then, thirteen years after her operation, the sky began to fall again, this time in the form of a fever.

I knew that the fever and fatigue her daughter described to me over the phone might be ominous. People with artificial valves are more vulnerable than usual to an infection of the heart's lining called "endocarditis." The infection is inherently difficult to cure because the "foreign body" of the valve interferes with complete healing of the tissues. Cultures of her blood grew out bacteria: her heart, most likely the artificial valve itself and the surrounding aorta, was indeed infected. She'd have to be hospitalized for several weeks in order to receive antibiotics in her veins around the clock.

At first, her fever did come down, haltingly, and I began to hope that we might have a chance. Over the next three weeks in the hospital, she felt gradually stronger; her appetite returned. Later, she was able to stroll around the ward, with the plastic intravenous line dangling from her arm, the IV pole rolling along at her side.

A month into her long treatment, though, her daughter called me one evening to say that her mother's blood pressure had fallen precipitously. Mrs. Corrigan had gone into shock and the doctor on call was worried. I was worried too. I suspected that the site of the resistant infection in her aorta had begun to leak, spilling blood into her chest cavity. If that was true, then the next few minutes would tell the story. Within those few minutes, the doctor called me back to say that Mrs. Corrigan was gone.

In the poem I began after my first visit to her house, I specifically recalled

> the royal plastic soldier
> whose body fills with whiskey
> and marches on a music box
>
> *How Dry I Am . . .*

But memory served me wrong. The soldier was *not* plastic but ceramic, a tall Horse Guard in a blue tunic with a red vest and cape and a tall brown hat. I'm sure about these details now: after Mrs. Corrigan died, her daughter gave me the music box as a gift.

More than twenty years have passed since I first saw Mrs. Corrigan, this tiny woman with her twin baggage of chest pain and dizziness. She had thirteen good years, vital ones, free of those symptoms. For that, both she and I were grateful. But I'm grateful to her for more than that.

Mrs. Corrigan was, for me, a living seminar in aortic valve disease, breathing proof that to study and know one patient well is often better than studying a hundred patients less thoroughly. Over the years, I touched her body again and again, during which time she taught me, tacitly, what a privilege it is to touch another's body, whether in the name of science or love. She was a tutor whose lessons were administered with grace and affection, lessons I've transferred gratefully to the care of many subsequent patients. One measure of the abiding impression she made on me is that seven years after the fact of her death, I can't bring myself to remove her name and address—or her chart—from my office files.

◈

From the Listening End
of the Stethoscope

◈

He calls my office late Friday afternoon to say that his heart has been running away with him all day. He's thirty-five and has had an artificial aortic valve in place for twelve years. Out of curiosity, I ask him to place the mouthpiece of his phone firmly against his chest wall. I listen closely: the clicks of his artificial valve are easy to hear. His heart rate is very rapid, about 180 beats a minute, and grossly irregular. The diagnosis is clear: He has a rhythm disturbance called "atrial fibrillation." I tell him that I'll phone in a prescription for him. He's to pick it up on his way home, take three of the tablets, and call me back in an hour or so. It's dark outside when the phone rings, but the news is good—a few minutes ago, abruptly, his heart slowed and the sense of "fluttering" in his chest vanished. Over the phone, the clicks of his valve are slow and regular. I've never used the telephone as a kind of long-distance stethoscope before, but the technique worked beautifully. Over the miles between us, he and I are smiling as we say good night.

$\mathcal{M}$y stethoscope, by now, is an old friend. It is, after all, the one I bought in medical school, twenty-eight years ago, though it's been replaced several times over, part by worn-out part, like atoms of the body. The earpieces slip into my ears tightly, the sounds of the world diminish. I enter the cave-dark, tone-dense hollow of the chest and tune in to the mother heart. My patient is a mother and she's better this morning, but still very sick. I bend and listen. As I do, I am aware of the film of sweat over the bridge of her nose and a flaring of her nostrils related to the work of her breathing. Her heart tones remind me of a racehorse laboring for the finish line: "lup-*dup*-pah, lup-*dup*-pah," and so forth. This triple cadence, understandably, is called a "gallop rhythm," after the canter of a horse. It connotes heart failure: her heart is unable to pump all the blood that it receives and her lungs are congested. Her heart muscle, the pump itself, is sick and unlikely to get better. As I slip the stethoscope back into my pocket, there is no way for me to know that within two years, she will be dead, suddenly, at the age of forty-one.

But most songs heard by the stethoscope are not as sad. Some are quite happy.

The idea for the stethoscope came to a young man in France as he watched two children at play with a wooden baton; one child scratched his end of the stick while the other, holding the opposite end to his ear, listened expectantly for the scratching to be "telegraphed" to him. The young man's mellifluous name was René Théophile Hyacinthe Laënnec (*lan-eck*). During his short life (1781–1826), he made many contributions to medicine, but he is best known as the father of the stethoscope.

The Ur-stethoscope, in fact, was a rolled-up cylinder of paper improvised by Laënnec in 1816 to better examine an obese young woman with heart disease. Laënnec was impressed with his *cornet de papier*: "I was not a little surprised and pleased to find that I could thereby perceive the action of the heart in a manner much more clear and distinct than I had ever been able to do by the immediate application of the ear." Later, the instrument was crafted out of wood, a hole was bored through the baton to facilitate the passage of sound; and it was divided, for portability, into halves that could be screwed together.

Long before Laënnec, physicians listened to hearts by simply placing the ear directly on the patient's chest. But the technique was not utilized that often because of concerns about modesty and hygiene. Then came the stethoscope, one of the earliest instruments to be physically interposed between doctor and patient. Laënnec's invention, however, despite its rudimentary form, was like the modern version in one important way: There was a human being at either end. As Dr. Dickinson Richards insisted in 1962, to use the stethoscope, "the doctor has to be within thirty inches of the patient," close enough to ensure the intimacy and laying on of hands often said to be lacking in medicine today.

The modern stethoscope—the word derives from the Greek *stethos,* meaning "chest"—evolved with new knowledge about the physics of sound transmission. Thus, the tubing between doctor and patient is of a prescribed bore and length. The earpieces must fit snugly. On the other end, the "heads" of the stethoscope, usually two or occasionally three in number, filter the sound. The flat piece, the diaphragm, picks up high-pitched sounds; the domed piece, the bell, registers low frequencies.

What kinds of music, or noise, arrive at the listening

end of the stethoscope? The most common use of the instrument is in the measurement of blood pressure, as the arterial blood column strains to thump under the cuff tightened around the arm. But the stethoscope is useful in decoding all the sounds of the body at work: the tick-tock of the fetal heart tones from the uterus; the rumblings of the gut under the abdominal wall (sounds that carry the aptly onomatopoeic Greek *borborygmos,* meaning "to rumble"); the rush of blood in narrowed vessels, notably the carotid arteries leading to the brain. In Laënnec's time, the stethoscope was most frequently employed to monitor the lungs: fully a third of the patients hospitalized in Paris were there because of tuberculosis. But the most dramatic use of it is in sorting out the cacophony of sound from the heart. Use of the stethoscope in this way is called "auscultation" (L. *auscultare,* "to listen").

The normal heart tones, a poet would note, are *iambic* in rhythm: a weaker followed by a stronger stress—lup-*dup,* lup-*dup.* These sounds, the "lup" and the "dup," are called the first and the second heart sounds, S-1 and S-2. They are due basically to the rhythmic paired closing of the four heart valves (tricuspid and pulmonary valves in the right side of the heart, mitral and aortic valves in the left side). The valves work gracefully and ingeniously to direct blood flow—from the right heart to the lungs, from the left heart to the body. The time between the *lup* and the *dup* defines systole (sis'toll-ee), the interval of contraction of the heart. The interval between the second sound and the subsequent first sound defines diastole (dye-as'toll-ee), the interval of relaxation. The flow of blood through the heart is often made turbulent (e.g., after exercise or with structural abnormalities of the heart); it is this turbulence that produces cardiac "murmurs." A murmur is often musical in character, and may occur in systole, diastole, or throughout both intervals, depending on the cause.

Many, perhaps most, heart murmurs are not pathological at all. An estimated 50 percent of all children, if their hearts are examined often enough, will have a murmur at some point. The turbulent blood flow in their active, growing bodies is one explanation of such "innocent" murmurs. These are the happiest sounds, joys to find. Similarly, many pregnant women develop murmurs as the torrential blood flow to the gravid uterus places an extra work-load on the maternal heart. The revved-up circulation that occurs with anemia or an overactive thyroid may also produce such murmurs.

But what of pathological murmurs? The valves of the heart may dysfunction for many reasons. Basically, dysfunction takes one of two forms: a narrowing of the valve ("stenosis") or a leakage ("insufficiency" or "regurgitation"). Stenosis of the aortic valve, situated between the left ventricle and the aorta, is a good example. With cardiac contraction, the three pliable leaflets of a normal valve are thrown open abruptly, like swinging doors, allowing blood to pass from the left ventricle to the aorta. After contraction, the leaflets recoil and close, halting any retreat of the aortic blood back into the ventricle. If the valve is narrowed by disease and scarring, however, the squeezing of blood through it may produce enough turbulence to cause a systolic murmur.

The loudness of murmurs is graded from 1 to 6 (6 is loud enough to be heard with the stethoscope completely off the chest). Rarely, a murmur is loud enough to be heard several feet away without using a stethoscope. Opening and closing "clicks" of certain artificial heart valves may be audible to others in a quiet waiting room.

A sense of rhythm is helpful in the interpretation of complex cardiac sounds. Generations of medical students, learning auscultation, have used a rhythmic, exaggerated pronunciation of the word *Ken-tuck-y, Ken-tuck-y,* to help time the gallops of the heart. Some conditions produce extra cardiac sounds: a variety of clicks, "rubs," and murmurs. Inflammation of the sac around the heart—pericarditis—results in a distinctive "scratchy" rub (the quality of the rub can be simulated by taking a small pinch of hair near the ear and rubbing the fingers together briskly). One of the most dramatic sounds in medicine is called "Hamman's crunch," after the physician who described its typical features. Auscultation of the heart after air has been introduced into the center of the chest (after a stab wound, for example) may reveal a crackling and crunching of the air and fluid around the beating heart, sounds that reminded Hamman (and thousands of clinicians since) of the crunch of snow under heavy boots.

Auscultation is usually done with the patient lying down. But listening with the patient sitting tilts the pendulous heart toward the chest wall, facilitating diagnosis. Listening with the patient standing, squatting, or with his feet elevated off the bed all may be used in special circumstances.

A complete examination of the lungs also includes auscultation: as the patient breathes deeply, air rushing through the bronchial tree may pass over abnormal fluid within the bronchi (in pneumonia, for example), causing soft bubbling sounds.

Another valuable technique for examination of the lungs (less valuable for the heart) is that of *percussion.* In percussion, the long finger of one hand is laid flat against the chest wall while the long finger of the other hand taps or percusses it. Changes in the quality or "timbre" of the thumping sounds thus generated can help detect abnormal collections of fluid at the base of the lungs. Leopold Auenbrugger (1722–1809), a Viennese physician, is the father of percussion; applying the technique to the human chest was suggested to him by wine testers who drummed their fingers over the kegs to check the level of fluid within them.

Years ago, as fledgling medical students in St. Louis, Luis Vasconez and I were assigned to examine the heart and lungs of a patient. While I stood in front of the (patient) patient, attempting to make sense out of his heart sounds,

Luis was trying out his newfound technique of percussion over the patient's back: Luis' drumbeats sounded like thunder in my stethoscope. Needless to say, the techniques of auscultation and percussion are not intended to be carried out simultaneously!

Despite the long history of the stethoscope, there is much more to learn about auscultation. Until the 1960s, for example, a click or clicks heard between the lup and the dup were thought to be noncardiac in origin. Sophisticated studies have now shown that such clicks often arise from the mitral valve in a condition called "mitral valve prolapse." *(See "Billows of the Heart" in Part Three.)* Newer techniques help us understand what we're hearing: these include echocardiography (viewing the heart with ultrasound) and magnetic resonance imaging, a noninvasive technique that gives clear views of cardiac anatomy without the injection of dyes. Thus, as the stethoscope keeps the physician near the bedside of the patient, its messages are continually reinterpreted in light of new information.

Recently, I and my older son, a medical student in Boston, spent a morning at the hospital decoding the heart sounds that emanated from a wondrous electronic teaching mannequin called "Harvey." Harvey can be programmed to simulate a wide variety of murmurs (and pulses). I envy my son the process of discovery that lies before him. It will take some time. Only with time, only after moving the stethoscope like a metal-detector over the landscape of countless hearts, does one truly learn how to be still and listen. Such training of the ear comes only with experience. The art of auscultation is remarkably like listening to Mozart's clarinet quintet—after so long a time, one is able to follow the voice of the cello and thus appreciate its individual music within the ensemble.

Physicians and patients, of course, are not the only ones interested in the arcane language of the heart. John Ciardi wrote a fine poem called "Lines From the Beating End of the Stethoscope." And W. H. Auden, in "Lay your sleeping head, my love," speaks knowingly of the "knocking heart."

The very first auscultator, surely, was a lover—head pillowed on the drum of the lover's chest—who heard the murmurs and murmurings of the heart and worried what they might mean long before—and long since—Laënnec.

◈

The Case of the Missing Pulses

◈

No one knew better than Arthur Conan Doyle the parallels between the work of a physician and that of a detective. Sherlock Holmes, in fact, was based on one of Doyle's medical school professors. Doyle finished his medical training in Edinburgh, then opened an office, but the patients were slow to come. There's a story that Doyle put a sign in his window that read SMALL FEVERS GRATEFULLY ACCEPTED. Whether or not that story is true, he did turn, early on, to writing. In 1885, Doyle completed his M.D. thesis; two years later came the first Holmes story, "A Study in Scarlet." Holmes's powers of observation and deduction are just as valuable when found in a physician. Moreover, the work of both physician and detective is rooted in the temporal and the palpable; it is the "real" world that excites them. Consider this statement from "The Red-Headed League": ". . . for strange effects and extraordinary combinations we must go to life itself, which is always far more daring than any effort of the imagination." Amen.

$\mathcal{T}$his is her thirteenth April. Puberty has barely touched her, in the same tentative way that spring first brushes the trees. She is a painting in process, a Monet perhaps, but even at this early stage, in this austere examining room, it's easy to tell that the finished portrait will be beautiful. I take her blood pressure. It's up: 140/90, high even taking into account that this visit with me could be stressful for her. I'm one of a very few doctors she's been checked by since she was an infant.

She comes from the Georgia mountains, north of Atlanta. When she was a few days old, a physician found a heart murmur—but he told the mother that it might be an "innocent" murmur that she might "outgrow." Her childhood has been generally healthy, although she has complained of leg cramps after vigorous exercise. But a few weeks ago, a public health nurse again heard a heart murmur and asked that she be seen by a doctor.

I check her pulses. The arteries bumping under the fingers are reassuring in their constancy: the two radial pulses at the wrist; the carotids in the neck, thumping to either side of the Adam's apple; and the femoral pulses at the top of the leg. *Wait*. Where is the right femoral pulse? The left? Any pulses at all in the feet? No. Not a trace. The diagnosis is taking shape: I measure the blood pressure in her legs—it's very low.

Coarctation of the aorta is basically a congenital *crimp,* a narrowing, in the long pipe of the aorta. The crimp occurs just after the arm vessels take off—hence the arm blood pressure is high, the pressure below the crimp, in the legs, is low. The body reacts to the narrowed aorta by dispatching blood *around* the coarctation, bypassing it just as drivers use side streets to bypass a traffic jam. The bypass is accomplished by *collateral* vessels, ones that are normally present (but smaller) and can be pressed into extra duty. So blood *does* get to the legs, but via a circuitous route and in decreased amounts—hence, no femoral pulses. With exercise, her legs get too little blood—thus, her legs cramp.

On the girl's chest X ray, there is evidence of collateral blood flow: her intercostal (rib) arteries, carrying much-increased amounts of blood around the coarctation, have actually eroded the bone as they pulsate, a sign known as "rib-notching." I am now convinced that she has coarctation—and that we can help her. I draw a picture for her and her mother. I ask that they return to see me in a month, after one more relatively new (and painless) test that can be done as an outpatient. Mother and daughter will have a lot to talk about on their drive back to the mountains.

Like all other causes of high blood pressure, coarctation increases the risk of stroke, heart failure, and premature death. Early diagnosis and treatment are important. For decades, the only way to gauge the severity of the coarctation was to do a cardiac catheterization. This requires a hospital stay and the threading of a catheter into the aorta, then injection of a dye that throws the narrowing into relief. But in recent years, we have also been able to use what is called magnetic resonance imaging—MRI—with far greater ease and exquisite definition of cardiac anatomy. The painless nature of MRI makes it especially useful in pediatric heart cases.

MRI, originally called nuclear magnetic resonance (NMR), dates from the mid-1940s and the work of Felix Bloch and Edward Purcell (who received the Nobel prize for it in 1952). They studied the reactions of protons, particles in the nuclei of atoms, to a strong magnetic field that is intermittently "pulsed" with radio waves. MRI depends on the fact that protons, under such conditions, will absorb and emit the radio signals, which can then be analyzed by a computer. MRI was initially used to define the molecular structures of substances. But because protons, in the form of hydrogen ions, are present throughout the body (in water, for example), MRI was tested on the body. In 1976, a finger was "imaged"; there followed an explosion of medical interest. (The original name for the technique, nuclear magnetic resonance, was dropped in 1984 because the word *nuclear,* which referred to the role played by the atomic nucleus, gave the incorrect impression that radiation, which might have harmful side effects, was being emitted.)

As I enter the control room, an eight-year-old boy with congenital heart disease has just reclined on the table that slides quietly into the MRI machine in the next room. A huge (twelve feet tall) metal doughnut contains the superconducting magnet; the wiring inside is cooled, with liquid nitrogen and helium, to near zero degrees. An electrical current introduced into the wire under such conditions will flow with minimal resistance and produce a magnetic field thousands of times greater than the earth's.

In the control room, I am outside the magnetic field. I can see images of the boy's heart on monitors. The MRI reconstructs "slices" in several different planes. Each tissue has a special shade within the white-gray-black continuum—fat is white, lungs black, heart muscle gray. Radio waves are now being pulsed into the magnetic field; the pulses, in bursts of six, are close together and loud, like the firing of a machine gun. Because the noise alone could disturb the child, he wears headphones during the study. I try to imagine how I'd react to being inside the long body-tunnel of the MRI. If an eight-year-old can do it, surely I can; I resolve to try out the machine myself.

The clear three-dimensional image of the boy's heart

shows a large hole between the two lower chambers—a ventricular septal defect. Also, the great vessels that leave the heart (one to the lungs, the other to the body) have been somehow switched or transposed during embryonic development. Correction of these defects will be a major surgical procedure, one that requires the most meticulous pre-op study. But we are all pleased that surgery will help him.

Above the control panel is a Mickey Mouse hat with plastic ears—and a stuffed animal for even younger patients. Either object could acompany a small patient into the MRI because they contain no metal. Iron-based metals (which could come under the magnet's power) are a no-no within the magnet room. A metal detector like those at airports is used to screen patients—but the medical history is the most important tool for screening. Pacemakers and small vascular clips used in neurosurgery pose the biggest potential hazards; disruption of a clip, for example, might trigger bleeding inside the head.

The technician tells me of a harrowing experience she had a year ago. She wheeled a patient into the MRI room, thinking the patient was outside the magnetic field. As the patient stood up, the technician turned the metal wheelchair a bit, exposing a greater surface area to the magnet. With that, the wheelchair was pulled, with awesome force and speed, toward the magnet, and crashed into it. Anyone in the path of the chair could have been seriously injured. Fortunately, no one was. In the control room there is a button for such an eventuality. Called the "Emergency Quencher," it's a mechanism to immediately shut down the magnet (which otherwise is never shut off). Pushing this button automatically costs someone $10,000—to reset the magnet.

The eight-year-old, inside the MRI for over an hour, has done very well, but now says he has to go to the bathroom. The technician cajoles him to hold on just a bit longer: "We're almost through." MRI studies often *do* take a long time. The two MRI machines here study a total of about twenty patients per day; 70 percent are neurological cases, the rest cardiac, abdominal, and orthopedic.

Not only static images are available from the MRI—since radio waves bounce back in contrasting configurations from the heart and from the blood inside it, actual flow can be depicted when the heart's action is pieced together on "movies" by computer. No dye, such as that used in cardiac catherization, need be injected. But there are certain things the MRI *cannot* do, such as measurement of pressures, an integral part of a cath. An echocardiogram (using ultrasound waves) is simpler, quicker, and cheaper than MRI, and very useful. The truth is, an MRI, a cath, an echocardiogram, are all different, complementary ways of looking at the same elephant, the punctual or dilatory heart.

The young boy, smiling, hops down from the MRI bed and is led off to the bathroom. The radiologist and I take all the metal out of our pockets, including our credit cards (which the MRI would erase), then enter the room. Light and airy, it's a large space, but clearly dominated by the machine. On one wall is a huge mural, a nature scene, the last thing one sees before being slid into the long tube of the MRI, the opening of which is a circle about three feet in diameter. Determined to experience what my patients do, I stretch out, a pillow under my knees for comfort. I put on special glasses—they cost $1,100—that allow me to see, via a tilted mirror on the frames, back over the top of my head while I'm reclining. Thus, I can maintain visual contact, at least, with the outside world. It *does* help that the tube is open at both ends. Still, as the bed slides in (on my signal), there is a definite feeling of confinement. I am much larger than the little boy—especially in girth. I remember what the technician told me: "I never knew so many people were claustrophobic before I took this job." And the radiologist's words: "I've been in there eighty or ninety times; now I just go right off to sleep." The air is warm with the child's recent sweat and breathing, the atmosphere "close." I feel as

though I've landed right in the middle of a short story by
Edgar Allan Poe. Or like Stone the Magnificent Human
Cannonball, about to be shot from a cannon while the
crowd oohs and aahs. It's easy to see why four or five of the
twenty patients studied here each day benefit from being
sedated. I'm glad I don't have to lie here for an hour—after
only a few minutes, I'm ready to be pulled out, back into
the real world, out of the inner circle of magnets and
protons.

I and my young north Georgia patient with coarctation
now have a journey in common, one through the tunnel of
the MRI. The images of her heart are now ready to view.

From the side, the aorta looks like a large question
mark—it rises gracefully out of the heart, curves upward to
give off vessels to the head and arms, then descends along
the spine toward the lower body. We are primarily interested in the aorta, but her MRI is an object lesson in the
anatomy of the entire upper body. The trachea, dividing
into the bronchi for the two lungs. The humerus, socketed
into the shoulder joint. And the tributaries of bile and blood
within the liver. All of this amazes me, just as surely as it
would have amazed my grandfather, a general practitioner.

Her coarctation is easily seen on the MRI movies. The
narrowing in her aorta is severe, but discrete and short. We
get a clear idea of how the surgeon can cut out the narrowed
area and join the ends of the aorta together. Medical mercy
really does arrive often now in many forms: one is that after
this youngster's surgery, her legs will not cramp as she
walks up, down, and around her Georgia mountain.

◈

The Wolf Inside

◈

One summer evening in 1981, near Rome's Trevi Fountain, I was surprised to see, on the brightly lit marquee of a nearby movie, the words *La Saggezza nel Sangue,* and, in parentheses below, the translation, *Wise Blood.* I felt as though I'd bumped into an old friend. Sure enough, when I searched the advertising posters outside the theater, I found the name Flannery O'Connor, the great Georgia writer on whose work the movie is based. I never met Ms. O'Connor, though I likely would have had she lived out anything near her allotted biblical span. I photographed the marquee for my slide collection. I tossed several coins into the fountain—enough for both of us.

$\mathcal{F}$our weeks before she died of a complication of lupus erythematosus, Flannery O'Connor wrote, in a letter dated July 5, 1964, "The wolf, I'm afraid, is inside tearing up the place. I've been in the hospital 50 days already this year." By the time of her next recorded letter three days later, she had received the rite of extreme unction. I never met Flannery O'Connor, but I never see a patient with lupus now without thinking of those words and of the woman herself.

The word *lupus* was appropriated whole to the medical vocabulary directly from the Latin meaning "wolf." This autoimmune system disease affects virtually every organ in the body. About 60 percent of patients will have a red ("erythematous") rash on the face, over the bridge of the nose, and on the cheeks below the eyes, in a more or less "butterfly" pattern, a shape similar to the facial markings of a wolf.

I saw a young woman with lupus today. She doesn't have the rash. She does have extensive kidney disease and, according to an X ray, a massively enlarged heart. Hers is a dramatic case: In just two months, she has gained fifty pounds, all of it water. I go up to her bed, introduce myself, and shake her hand. As she tells her story, it's obvious that she is reasonably comfortable. She's breathing easily, her blood pressure and pulse are good. Since I was first asked to see her, I have also learned that, despite the chest X ray, her heart is not enlarged. Rather, the pericardial sac around it, designed to hold a scant ounce of fluid, has managed to stretch hugely, accumulating perhaps three quarts of fluid—thus the enlarged heart shadow on her X ray. She is waterlogged, her tissues swimming in excess fluid that her diseased kidneys cannot excrete. The echocardiograph is like a sonar unit, its echo like the sonogram of a fetus: but instead of a fetus floating within its sac of liquid, there was her heart, normal in size, bobbing and squeezing like a fist.

Her kidney disease is such that she is losing huge amounts of protein in the urine. Normal kidneys are designed to filter the total blood volume selectively many times each day, manufacturing, in the process, several quarts of urine while losing only tiny amounts of protein from the blood that has been filtered. But her kidneys are leaking protein like a sieve. Without that protein to hold the plasma within the blood vessels, she is leaking water into all her tissues, including the pericardial sac. After talking with her at length about her illness, I examine her. A soft, scratchy noise, synchronous with the heartbeat, confirms her inflamed pericardium, one of the problems often seen with lupus. Her legs are grossly swollen. I press my fingers gently into the skin over her shins—the tips of my fingers sink in as though they were poking the soft belly of the puffy little doughboy in the television ad. Several minutes later, as I leave, the deep pits are still there.

Prednisone, a form of cortisone, has been started. The hope is that, in massive doses, the drug will help seal the protein leaks of her kidneys, and that diuretics will mobilize the fifty pounds of excess fluid she has accumulated. The immediate question is whether to use a needle to draw off the fluid from around her heart. The danger is that the fluid will restrict and restrain the heart's action, like the cellophane wrapper on a box of valentine candy, and jeopardize its all-important pumping. I decide we should not attempt to remove the fluid now, reasoning that it will only reaccumulate: the dike has multiple holes in it—the water would only seep back in. The cardiology fellows working with me disagree: they are in favor of the needle. I argue that we should wait for the drugs to work. I worry about her as I go to sleep that night; it is often easier to *do* something, rather than wait, but it's not always best for the patient. We keep a sterile tray, with a long pericardial needle in it, at her bedside, just in case.

Flannery O'Connor had lupus for some fourteen years before she imagined the wolf tearing up the place. The disease had begun, in late 1950, with, as she spelled it, AWTHRITUS. Arthritis, or joint pain, is present in 90 percent of patients with lupus. Just as common is an overwhelming fatigue, often accompanied by fever, loss of appetite, and loss of weight. The exact cause of lupus is uncertain, but it is known that in the course of the disease, the body makes antibodies directed against its own organs, antibodies capable in turn of damaging the organs. The process amounts to a kind of immunological betrayal of its owner by the body, an absolute autoimmune revolution. Lupus is primarily a disease of women (90 percent of cases, with a peak incidence in the childbearing years). Flannery O'Connor's father died of lupus, however, and today, human lymphocyte antigen (HLA) typing, a kind of tissue "matching" that is done for organ transplants, confirms that there may be a genetic predisposition.

New forms of therapy, especially the judicious use of drugs to suppress the immune system, help slow progression of the disease, and also reduce the requirements for steroids, such as cortisone, with their side effects. Though lupus can be serious, the disease is also capricious, with both relapses and remissions: statistically, the majority of patients can look forward to a time when they are relatively free of problems.

Flannery O'Connor had a severe case: clearly, the "wolf" *was* inside. Sally Fitzgerald, editor of O'Connor's letters, speaks movingly of the time, late in 1950, when she learned from Flannery's mother "that Flannery was dying of lupus": "The doctor had minced no words. We were stunned. We communicated regularly with Mrs. O'Connor while she went through this terrible time and the days of uncertainty that followed, during Dr. Arthur J. Merrill's tremendous effort to save Flannery's life."

Dr. Merrill, Flannery's physician, is a former mentor of mine. About twenty years ago, he told me that Flannery's lupus was diagnosed just as more hopeful therapy became available (e.g., in 1949, P. S. Hench and co-workers reported the efficacy of ACTH and cortisone in arthritis). ACTH, a hormone that causes the body to secrete cortisone, was prescribed for Flannery in the early 1950s. The effect of ACTH (and cortisone, which she took later) is to blunt the body's response to the turncoat antibodies of lupus. The drugs worked—at a price. ACTH and cortisone can have significant side effects: thinning of bone (osteoporosis); loss of muscle strength; a moonlike shape to the face; exacerbation of duodenal ulcers; altered metabolism; increased susceptibility to infections; mood changes, ranging from a feeling of well-being to depression and even psychosis.

Flannery was well aware of the side effects as she wrote: "My dose of prednisone had been cut in half on Dr. Merrill's orders because the nitrogen content of the blood has increased by a third. So far as I can see, the medicine and the disease run neck & neck to kill you." But she felt better on the medications. In 1960, after ten years on steroids, she wrote that "as Dr. Merrill says, it is better to be alive with joint trouble than dead without it. Amen."

Over the next week, as I see my own young lupus patient, I can tell, thank God and prednisone, she is improving. She has lost more than thirty pounds, all of it water. The pericardial fluid has diminished—her echo looks better. She's going to make it. And she gives me a tired, heroic smile.

Heroic is, I think, the word for Flannery O'Connor too. When the disease struck her, she was twenty-five, a graduate of the Iowa Writers' Workshop, a fledgling writer just beginning to make a name for herself. Despite the wolf, the next fourteen years were productive ones for her. She won three O. Henry first prizes; the National Book Award came posthumously, in 1971. Many of her best short stories were written during these years: "A Good Man Is Hard to Find" in 1953; "Good Country People" in 1955; "Everything That Rises Must Converge" in 1961; "Revelation" in the spring of 1964, just months before she died.

Flannery O'Connor knew at least two kinds of isolation—that required by her craft and that imposed by her illness. Listen to her in 1956: "I have never been anywhere but sick. In a sense sickness is a place, more instructive than a long trip to Europe, and it's always a place where there's no company, where nobody can follow." Of course, in a metaphorical sense, Flannery O'Connor never stopped traveling. And the joy of discovery kept her at the typewriter. From one of the earliest of her collected letters (July 21, 1948), there is evidence that the process of writing was, for her, journey enough: "I have to write to discover what I am doing. Like the old lady, I don't know so well what I think until I see what I say."

Flannery O'Connor *endured,* to use Faulkner's term, despite the lupus. That she weathered the devastating side effects of ACTH and cortisone, continuing to write, slowly, painfully, to find out exactly what she *did* think, makes her a heroine to me. But then, many of my patients seem heroic to me, especially the ones with chronic illnesses.

Through its Latin root, the word *doctor* means "teacher"; but very often it is the patient who does the teaching, especially when the lesson is one in courage. It's one thing to have an acute, limited illness, to pass the bloody agonizing kidney stone and be done with it; it's quite another to go to sleep with pain, to dream that it's gone, then wake back up to the same pain waiting like a wild beast at the foot of your bed. And to persevere despite the pain, feeling it flow like electricity out of your forearms along your sore wrists and out to your stiff fingers to discover precisely how the twenty-six letters of the alphabet plan to marry *this* time.

Lupus betrayed Flannery O'Connor like a sophisticated Trojan horse, one with a wolf inside. Once within the body's gates, the enemy was everywhere. Still, she prevailed, even if it was only until her thirty-ninth year. And her life and words are a study in keeping on keeping on. It is in that spirit that I move to the next patient.

Listening to the Patient

The inventor of the stethoscope, Laënnec, knew that the medical history given by a patient is just as important—sometimes even more important—than the "lup-dup" of the patient's heart. Among his advice to physicians is: "Listen! Listen to your patient! He is giving you the diagnosis."

$\mathcal{I}$n a circle of light, we sit as witnesses: Gregor Samsa has just been changed into a giant beetle. In the opening sentence of Franz Kafka's *The Metamorphosis,* Gregor has awakened to find that he has been transformed into "a monstrous vermin." Our group now discussing Gregor's prognosis consists of medical types: faculty, residents, and students—plus two friends with Ph.D.'s in literature who keep us honest. But why are we reading the novella by Kafka in the first place? For one thing, like complicated patients, the story resists easy explanations and invites vigorous discussion. Its subtleties, its ambiguities, are not unlike those of our patients.

My conviction is that Gregor's plight parallels that of many people who have been disfigured or disabled by disease; they often feel just as isolated and alienated as Gregor. Prodding the group a bit, I suggest that there are at least three ways to view Gregor's metamorphosis: Gregor *thought* he was changed into a beetle; his *family and friends* thought he was changed into a beetle; or he *was* changed into a beetle.

Tonight, the students are in no mood for ambiguity: one speaks up with absolute confidence: "No problem. He really was changed into a beetle."

In the fall of 1982, a senior medical student who knew I was interested in writing came to my office to ask me to direct a new medical student elective in literature and medicine. I said yes immediately.

These seniors had already spent three rigorous years learning scientific medicine. What did they need literature for? In point of fact, the resonances between the two fields, between literature and medicine, are powerful, as one readily perceives in the works of a number of physician-writers: François Rabelais; Anton Chekhov, whom some regard as the world's greatest short story writer and playwright; Arthur Conan Doyle, who created Sherlock Holmes while waiting for his first patients; John Keats, who spent as much of his life, six years, studying medicine as he did writing poetry; Peter Roget, who compiled his *Thesaurus* after retiring from medicine; W. Somerset Maugham, who interned at the same hospital as John Keats, but some seventy-five years after Keats; William Carlos Williams, the pediatrician who changed the face of American poetry; and contemporaries such as Walker Percy and Lewis Thomas.

Physicians and writers draw upon the same source: the human encounter, people and their indelible stories. And the works of both depend on skillful use of the senses. As with Holmes, success rests with the powers of observation.

Our literature-and-medicine elective is part of a gentle revolution in medical education that began, in part, as a reaction to the intensity, the inevitable encroachment of modern technology. Technology, as crucial as it has become to medical care, always threatens to intrude on the intimacy of the doctor–patient relationship. No one wants to dispense with technology, only to distance it and keep it in context; literature can be especially helpful in this.

Literature, indeed, can have a kind of *laboratory* function. In other words, the medical ear must be properly trained to hear stories—a medical history, after all, is a short story. In this sense, a person's life can be thought of as a series of stories, coalescing over time to form the most idiosyncratic novel ever written. The good doctor must learn to listen for the real messages in these stories of his patients, to read them, as Robert Frost used to say, "with a listening ear."

When Tolstoy, in *The Death of Ivan Ilyich*, details the final illness of a high court judge, it is a story that every seasoned physician has encountered, but one that each student has to learn. And Tolstoy is a superb teacher. Ivan's problems begin innocuously enough: a slip on a stepladder and a blow to his flank. "A strange taste in his mouth and some discomfort in his left side" lead him to consult a doctor. Ivan wants only to know if his condition is serious; the physician, imperious and remote, is preoccupied with the diagnostic possibilities: "a floating kidney, chronic catarrh, or disease of the caecum"—one of Tolstoy's few slipups, since the cecum (the modern spelling) is on the *right* side.

The reader—and Ivan Ilyich—are made aware of the seriousness of Ivan's condition through the eyes of his brother-in-law, who has not seen Ivan for some time: "His brother-in-law opened his mouth to gasp, but checked himself . . ." "What is it—have I changed?" "Y-yes . . . you have." Ivan has only to compare his face in the mirror with a recent photograph to know how ominous his illness is: "It's not a question of a caecum or a kidney, but of life and . . . death."

Ivan's downhill course closely parallels the "stages" described in 1969 by Elisabeth Kübler-Ross in her book *On Death and Dying*. But Ivan, by now, is no abstraction: he is one of us, one of our patients or family. We hurt with him. We are relieved when his agony is over. Once in Tolstoy's grasp and seized by this story, the medical student is well on the way to a deeper understanding of what it is like to be dying. Literature will help lead a young doctor, if the physician permits, to the proper sensitivity; it will help to find the proper words for the proper moment, even to place the doctor, vicariously, in the patient's hospital bed.

Literature can provide for students of medicine something of what psychotherapy can provide for its patients: catharsis, personal insights, and support. The senior year of medical school is a time in which students can look both backward and forward over their careers. What happens in our study group is this: We *begin* by talking about a novel or a poem, but we often come around to discussing *our own lives*. We don't *intend* this; it just happens. Literature thus becomes a vehicle for much-needed reflection.

Critics will say that such "extracurricular" reading ought to have been done in college. I understand that point of view. But I submit that a student's reaction to a novel read *before* medical training is often very different from his reaction to the same novel read *after* such training. Moreover, literature is *not* extracurricular—it speaks directly to what many physicians actually do in practice. Literature is hard data, not soft.

Literature is also valuable because it provides *opportunity for ethical reflection*. In the dark irony of Jorge Luis Borges's story "The Immortals"—written, bear in mind, well before the advent of the artificial heart—a man consults a gerontologist, Dr. Raul Narbondo, for a general checkup.

The smarmy Dr. Narbondo speaks: "The death of the body is a result, always, of the failure of some organ or other, call it the kidney, lungs, heart, or what you like." Narbondo has the easy answer to this problem—each organ can be replaced: "The body can be vulcanized and from time to time recaulked, and so the mind keeps going. Surgery brings immortality to mankind." In return, the "candidate transfers his property to us, and the Narbondo Company, Inc. . . . guarantees your upkeep . . . to the end of time." The patient, recoiling from this technological Faustian contract, is last seen in his hotel room, wearing a disguise and "setting down this account of the facts."

Borges shrewdly presaged our era, in which the replacement of defective hearts, kidneys, and other organs is, indeed, becoming commonplace. But is the story not also a cautionary tale, warning the physician against both arrogance and uncritical espousal of technology? Narbondo deals in spare body parts without regard for quality of life.

I regret, myself, that I did not read *The Plague,* by

Albert Camus, until I was forty. Camus had the genius to couch his searching philosophical questions in a most palatable form, the novel. The book's *sforzando* opening is stunningly direct: "When leaving his surgery on the morning of April 16, Dr. Bernard Rieux felt something soft under his foot. It was a dead rat. . . ."

Camus then chronicles the devastation of an Algerian town by bubonic plague. As is often the case, the metaphorical scope of the novel extends well beyond its literal text: the "plague" today could as well be AIDS, or cancer, or heart disease. Indeed, for everyone who reads it, there is, in the Algerian town of this great novel, the very isolation, the lack of communication, the terror, the experience and the feel of death that may well accompany all serious illnesses.

A student has just left my office, having dropped off a poem for me to look at. It was written for him by one of his patients, a nine-year-old girl hospitalized for treatment of a recurrent malignancy (her prognosis is good). Her poem, about frogs and crickets, spring and its beginnings, reminds me not to overlook one other obvious attribute of literature: The writing of it can be therapeutic in and of itself. Her little gift, complete with a lipsticked kiss at the top of the page, is emblematic of the healing word.

We sit in a circle of light, witnesses. The seniors will soon be gone, expected harvest and annual loss. In his poem "The House Was Quiet and the World Was Calm," Wallace Stevens asserts, "The reader became the book." Something like that has happened around this circle. We have listened hard for the voices of Tolstoy, Kafka, and others, in moments as intimate and expectant as a séance.

But the real spirits we keep hoping to reach are our own.

◈

PART TWO
*The Patient
as Art*

◈

An Infected Heart

Lovers have always known that love can go bad and infect the metaphorical heart. And physicians have long known that love can infect the literal heart, too. My first palpable encounter with the literal heart, early in medical school, in gross anatomy lab, showed me just how resistant such infections can be.

The body on which we worked was that of a man, perhaps fifty years old. He was muscular, in life a laborer, I imagined. His body was like a textbook, perfect, flawless. As freshman medical students, we had no idea why such a perfect body might have died—until we opened the chest.

His heart, like his other muscles, was heavy with the weight of life. But the most striking abnormality within the cave of his chest was the enlargement of his aorta, the artery that distributes blood over the body. His aorta was ballooned out, swollen to three times its normal size. Such a weak, bulging aorta, an aneurysm, could have come only from syphilis, which he had contracted years—or, more likely, decades—before. This revelation completely transformed our daily encounters with our cadaver. This was now no longer a mere anatomy textbook, yielding up its slow secrets. No. This was a man, instantly humanized, who had walked and worked among us and died of love. And, in some metaphysical sense, the woman from whom he had contracted the disease was still there with him on the dissection table, after all those years. As Racine wrote in *Phèdre*, "It is no longer a passion hidden in my heart; it is Venus herself fastened to her prey."

$\mathcal{I}$ saw him first in April on cardiology consultation rounds. I was working with two emergency medicine residents and two cardiology fellows that month, swooping all over the hospital to see patients with suspected or clear-cut heart disease. The call over the beeper was from the burn unit.

We entered the sanctum of the unit through the swinging doors. Signs on the wall confronted us: DID YOU WASH YOUR HANDS? We did. And donned the gowns, masks, and puffy surgeon's caps that were required for the unit. We began to review the chart.

The man was young—maybe twenty-five years old—and had been burned—widely, severely. The surgeons had struggled for weeks to try to cover the burned areas with skin grafts before his wounds could be irreversibly infected. He'd been in the hospital since January—almost four months now. I thought of how much it hurts to burn a finger on a hot stove, then tried mentally to magnify it.

We listened as one of the fellows took the history: How had he been burned? The patient told us he'd been walking late one night in January when he spotted the distinctive orange glow and thick smoke of a major fire in a building he passed. He knocked loudly on the door and yelled for help. A young boy appeared at an upstairs window. The patient told us he broke in the door, roused the family out, then went back in for the boy. He'd saved the boy but had been badly burned in the process.

The man—his name was Robert—was sitting upright in a high-backed wheelchair. His limbs, abdomen, and back were swathed in bandages; he sat propped up on foam so as to put as little pressure as possible on the tender skin underneath. From a distance, his face reminded me of one painted by Rouault: dark, broad brushstrokes outlining it, another dark stroke lending prominence to the nose, and lighter tones for the rest of the face. Up close, the landscape of his face was made up of glistening caramel-colored islands of partially melted tissue; they were separated by—and seemed to be eroded by—the angry channeling red pigment of his blood that looked ready to well up at any moment from beneath the burned skin. The effect was that of a variably cooling recent lava flow. But that was not the most striking aspect of his countenance: his eyes had the look of pure terror, pupils dilated, lids widely separated—the eyes that everyone in medicine sees sooner or later. They lent to his face the unmistakable appearance of someone who's seen death and been changed by it.

We examined Robert's heart. It was racing: 160 beats a minute. There was a soft heart murmur: "PfffFF . . . TT, PfffFF . . . TT, PfffFF . . . TT." Not loud, but not normal either, we decided among ourselves.

Robert had done surprisingly well for several weeks as his own good skin was grafted over the burned areas. But then infection had set in. Antibiotics were started—first one, then two, then another set, as the bacteria became resistant to the drugs. The spiking daily fevers began—and drenching sweats. Cardiology was called to see him after bacteria were cultured from his blood. *Does he have endocarditis?* asked the consultation note.

We decided to do an echocardiogram. The machine was trundled up from the sixth floor of the hospital and set up in the room. An echocardiogram harks back to the sonar units used by submarines—the ones we all saw at the movies on Saturday afternoons while we were growing up, blithely unaware of any hearts but our own. The echo machine uses ultrasound waves, as does sonar, bouncing the waves off the interior anatomy of the body. Using the echo, one can visualize the heart's perpetual energy and, within it, in the swirling sea of blood, the graceful heart valves keeping the blood flowing straight and full speed ahead.

Robert's valves all looked normal, thin but with great tensile strength, smoothly opening and closing, all except the mitral valve. Instead of smoothly dancing in place, the mitral valve's motions were weighed down by a mass of heavy echoes that could mean only one thing: the blood- and bacteria-laden abnormal appendages of endocarditis. His heart was infected, all right, seeded from his infected burns and then itself constantly reseeding all parts of the body in its natural centrifugal energy. We were trapped and so was Robert. We might have had a better chance to cure the endocarditis had we not had the infected burns to contend with. As it was, the situation was a desperate one. We wrote out our orders and tried to explain the dilemma to Robert, being as optimistic as possible.

We saw Robert daily over the next two weeks. At first, by switching to yet another, more toxic, set of antibiotics, we seemed to be making some progress. His temperature came down—for four days it was almost normal. All the while the surgeons worked to cover his burns with grafts. They didn't take. Robert was given several transfusions of blood. But his kidneys were beginning to fail. We adjusted the medications, meeting incessantly to decide how to approach each new crisis. I could tell we were losing ground. Robert looked weaker and more resigned on each of our successive visits. The raging fever returned. He was going out in a blaze, an inferno of infection.

Several days later, as the group of us approached the door of Robert's room, we saw that he had a visitor. The visitor's back was toward us, but his gown was open. His suit was black, and above the tie-strings of the gown around his neck, we could see the white collar of the priesthood. We backed quietly out of the room and waited. In a few minutes, the priest came out, closing his Bible as he approached us, a silver cross dangling from a broad white ribbon folded over his forearm. We nodded to his nod. We examined Robert. He looked exhausted. There was a rosary in his hand. He barely noticed that we were in the room.

That afternoon, the cardiology team got an emergency call to the unit. As we arrived, donning our apparel quickly, we found the entire surgical team gathered around Robert's bed, always a bad sign. Robert had had a seizure, then his heart had skipped, shuddered, and stopped. Despite our efforts, there was no way to save him. For my part, I wasn't at all sure that Robert *wanted* to be saved any longer. I thought about our sessions in ethics class on "quality of life." Robert had had little of that in the last few months.

As we left the room a deputy sheriff outside approached us. He asked about Robert. We told him what had happened, that we'd lost the battle. It was only then that we learned the truth about Robert. Robert, said the deputy, was an arsonist. He had set blazes in two parts of a building back in January. But he'd gotten trapped between the two fires, was badly burned, and had barely escaped with his life by jumping from a second-story window. Robert's tale about his heroism, the young boy he'd saved, was a total lie, something he'd wanted us to believe and, in the haze of morphine, may have begun to believe himself. Ordinarily, he would have been placed under an around-the-clock guard, said the deputy; but, as he told us, "In his condition, he wasn't goin' no place."

We shrugged out of our gowns, shaking our heads in disbelief. We'd been had, all right. Robert must have figured that things would go better for him medically if his doctors thought he was a hero and not an arsonist. I like to think that knowing the truth about Robert wouldn't have affected our efforts to save him. But who can be sure of that? Robert couldn't.

Discovery:
The Case of Bryan

When I was growing up in Jackson, Mississippi, one particular doctor there was said to be an especially good diagnostician, *the* person to see if you'd been seized by some mysterious malady. Being a diagnostician has never been easy; today it's even harder because knowledge in medicine is accruing at such a rapid rate. Still, excellent diagnosticians can still be found and I know why. Though the work of such physicians is demanding, though they must work hard simply to *stay* educated, there are great rewards. The moment of diagnosis, especially the diagnosis of a problem that one can help, brings with it an exhilaration without equal. But, as Dr. Wilfred Trotter surmised, "Disease often tells its secrets in a casual parenthesis," which means you have to keep watching it all the time, lest you miss something that seems trivial but may be all-important.

$\mathcal{R}$ecently I was invited to speak before a group of educators who are especially concerned, in their professional lives, with what has been called *remedial education*. I said yes as soon as I saw my schedule was open: I've always had a hankering to talk about remedial education with some experts on the subject. I'm a kind of expert myself: my remedial education began as soon as I got out of school. I have a notion, a bias, you might say, that, in the largest sense, *all education is remedial*. Consider the world before and after Archimedes: you remember that Archimedes discovered the law of physics that reads, "A body in water will displace a volume of water that is equal to the body's volume." Archimedes is said to have discovered this principle in the act of taking his own bath, the body in question being his own. And he was so excited that he ran naked through the streets, shouting, "Eureka," which is Greek for "I found it."

At the onset of *Eureka,* at the moment when the water is still lapping the sides of Archimedes's bathtub, at that moment of *dis*-covery, the new information is unknown to anyone but the bather—who is, so to speak, quite beside himself. The rest of the world is oblivious to such moments: it reads the newspaper, borrows a cup of sugar, has the oil changed, or dozes to television. Nevertheless, the world has always been ready to receive the word at whatever high spot the imagination comes down the mountain with it. *Then,* books and lives are changed, as the world comes to grips with the new information. That's what I mean by education—or, more properly, remedial education. Educators are always fighting against the *double whammy of progress*: the other side of the coin of *knowledge* is the blank and open face of *ignorance*. Not that ignorance should be thought of categorically as a *bad* thing: it can't be all that bad because it's so common—as Will Rogers reminded us, "We are all ignorant, but on different subjects."

Medicine, it seems to me, is the discipline par excellence for remedial education. There is such burgeoning of ideas in medicine, such a plethora of research, so many new drugs, that it doesn't take the long sleep of a Rip van Winkle to get behind. Let me illustrate with a case in point.

Just about twenty years ago, as providence will sometimes work, I was assigned, as part of my Public Health Service duties, to a wondrous institution called Aidmore Hospital in Atlanta. In 1965 its halls rang with the shouts and horseplay of young patients: children with acute rheumatic fever, Sydenham's chorea (Saint Vitus' dance), congenital heart disease, and a wide variety of orthopedic problems. The patients ranged in age from infancy to the late teens. It was my privilege to be one of the physicians there. I'd had two years of training in internal medicine, no specific training as yet in cardiology, but I knew that cardiology was what I wanted to do.

I was on hand when the patient arrived from south Georgia with a diagnosis of myocarditis. The child was small, about three years old, his nostrils flaring with the work of breathing, but happy in spite of his severe cardiac problem. He played around the wards with his newfound friends, sailed on the swing set in the play area in back of the hospital, and seemed, on the surface, to be a normal child. But his parents knew better. He'd already had several episodes of pneumonia, which, with his cardiac disability, had rendered him small for his age. And he did have to work hard to keep up with the other kids.

His X ray told the story: His heart was large, in fact huge. And the physical examination and electrocardiogram showed no evidence of any heart disease that could be helped by cardiac surgery. The fault lay with the heart muscle itself: his cardiac pump was weak, flabby, incapable of keeping up with the needs of a growing child. And even more poignantly, his heart disease was likely to cause death within a few years. The only treatment we knew to try, in addition to the usual digitalis and diuretics, was that of *bed rest*—and how does one keep a three-year-old in bed beyond his dreaming, keep him *still* for any period of time, in order to rest his heart? We tried steroids, those nonspecific anti-inflammatory marvels—and we hoped for the best. We were ignorant in those days, but, then, we're *still* ignorant, in many ways, about heart muscle disease in most of its forms.

One afternoon, I decided to examine Bryan in order to check his progress. The nurse told me he was taking a nap. I expected to find him in his bed, sawing logs as only an afternoon napper can. And he was asleep—but the *sounds* he made while sleeping were those I'd expect from a slumbering baby walrus: more snorts and snores and inspiratory noise I've never heard from a human. I watched and listened in awe for several minutes. Even the intercostal muscles bridging his ribs moved inward with his labored respiratory efforts. I slid my stethoscope along his chest. It was difficult even to be sure there *was* a heart there—only at the end of expiration, as his lungs collapsed toward the next difficult breath, could I hear the "lup-dup-puh, lup-dup-puh, lup-dup-puh" of his valiantly straining, indeed, galloping, heart, trying its best to pass for normal. Then the heart tones were drowned out by the grunting, ubiquitous machinery of his breathing.

One of the most important duties of the cardiologist, in any given patient, is to exclude *reversible* forms of heart disease. There are many therapies for the ailing heart, but it's a cardiologist's dream to identify a single factor that is causing the problem—to find and remove that factor and rejoice while the patient recovers. Listening to Bryan's breathing constituted an epiphany for me.

It was at that point that my brain said, "Eureka," that the incandescent light bulb of insight and intuition went on in my head. I'd read in a medical journal, only a few weeks before, about partial upper airway obstruction secondary to huge tonsils and adenoids—and how such obstruction can lead to heart disease of otherwise unfathomable type. None of this was taught in medical school—though the reasoning behind it, including the colorful description of that patho-physiology designated as "Pickwickian" (after Dickens), was understood (see p. 112). Bryan fit the bill, at least partially: He was only a few years old and he was black, the two diagnostic markers we knew to look for. But *all* kids have big tonsils and adenoids, don't they? I shook Bryan, gently—he roused and sat up slowly with a sheepish, sleepish smile. As he struggled awake the snorting character of his breathing improved noticeably. I asked him to pant like a puppy dog (to take his mind off the tongue depressor), aiming my penlight. There they were, in all their lymphoid otherworldly ugliness and utility: the biggest set of tonsils I'd ever seen. They completely filled the back of his throat. I said, "Thanks, Bryan," and let him go back to his snoring while I lit out for the medical library to find that article.

The story shortens here. His cardiac catheterization showed huge swings in his elevated pulmonary artery pressures as a result of his respiratory efforts—and the diagnosis was made. An ENT (ear, nose, and throat) man then took the matter in hand. With the removal of Bryan's tonsils and adenoids, his heart disease left, too, and for good. We sent Bryan back to south Georgia on no medications, his heart size and function destined to be normal.

I like to think now of Bryan at age twenty-two, coasting around the bases after a home run or being inducted into Phi Beta Kappa. I also like to think of him a few decades from now, telling his grandchildren the implausible, but true, story of a certain anonymous little boy who was very ill with heart disease until his doctors realized, in the nick of time, that he had an ENT problem in cardiac camouflage.

Those culprits, big tonsils and adenoids, have doubtless been present since the first prehistoric man sneezed in response to the first viral upper respiratory infection. And they've doubtless been responsible for much heart disease over the millennia. Now that we understand this relationship, this new information must be disseminated, taught not only to our generation but to the next and the next, ad infinitum. Once a truth is discovered, the world must never be allowed to forget it. *That,* I submit, is remedial education, too, in its best and most important clothes.

I'm pleased to note, as I told my audience of remedial educators, that the word *remedy* is, at its etymological base, a *medical* word. It comes out of the Latin through the Anglo-French to the Middle English, from *re* plus *mederi,* which means "to heal." Remedial education, then, is healing at its root, branch, fruit, and leaf—and therein is its continuing joy.

The Timeless Heart

Sudden death, for the cardiologist, is an electrical event—or, rather, a nonelectrical one. In perhaps 20 percent of such cases, the heart simply "stops short," like the grandfather clock in the old song. Most often, death comes in the form of chaotic squiggles on the EKG, accompanied by a writhing motion of the heart that pumps no blood at all. This electrical disarray is called "ventricular fibrillation." It is *reversible* if an electrical shock (a defibrillation) is applied within a few minutes after the fibrillation begins. Hundreds of thousands of lives have been saved by quick use of the defibrillator. A person brought back from such a harrowing experience is sometimes said to be an example of the "Lazarus syndrome," a reference, of course, to the biblical character who was raised from the dead.

$\mathcal{T}$here lived, not so long ago, in Brooklyn, two sisters and their father. When the older sister, Rachel, married, she did so with a mixture of joy and heartache because her husband had his business so far away. Nevertheless, she cleaved to him and moved her life to the small Mississippi town. Mornings, Rachel worked in their furniture store on Main Street. Afternoons she kept their home—a white, two-story, antebellum house, only two blocks from the store. In summer, white curtains whipped and sang at the windows. In winter, two huge oak trees stood their leafless guard in front of the house. And just as she would have done in the old country, Rachel wrote a letter every day to her sister, Hannah, in Brooklyn. And Hannah wrote back.

Every morning, in all weathers, Rachel sat at the breakfast table and wrote her letters. She dispatched them on flowered stationery out of the big white house toward Brooklyn. She told of her life in this strange new place. She spoke of sisterly, elemental things: the price of firewood, the merits of keeping one's own chickens; of barbecues, sawmills, the rare but tasty scandal that can be cooked up only on small-town stoves.

Hannah never married. After their father died, she continued to live in the brownstone on Dumas Street. She sat in the living room and wrote her older sister about the city and its noisy mysteries. About institutions that everyone agreed had to be timeless. The Brooklyn Dodgers. And Coney Island. And snow, light on the air, heavy on the shovel of the boy next door.

In time Rachel bore a son, Arthur, who was to be the first of three children. He learned the hills and valleys of Mississippi just as he would have learned, had he been raised in Brooklyn, its secrets, from Ebbets Field to the Bridge. And Arthur entered his mother's letters, which record that he did well at the university, that he married, that he and his wife had their own three children.

The Depression brought hard times to everyone. But those years were made almost intolerable for Rachel by the death of her beloved husband. Rachel said later that she would have died, too, but for the children. The family buried its father, then closed ranks; and Arthur took his father's place in the store.

But there was more sorrow not far away. Twelve short years after his father's death, Arthur fell into the clutches of angina. The pain came over his shoulder like a pair of pliers and Arthur was introduced to the mercies of nitroglycerin. Soon, Rachel found that even quiet talks with Arthur were interrupted so that he could place one of the small white tablets under his tongue. Long before his time, he began to look old. His angina worsened. One April day, he went gray in the face, and, only fifty-five, Arthur, too, left this world, suddenly, gracefully, in his sleep.

There was, then, no grief like Rachel's in all of Mississippi. News of Arthur's death spread as far as Jackson, where it was recorded in the papers. And he was buried. In those days, Mississippi was still a long way from Brooklyn. Hannah had no way of knowing of this tragedy. A week passed—two weeks—but there was no word from Rachel. Hannah was worried. Finally a letter came. Rachel explained that she had not been feeling well, but was stronger now; and once more she began to write to Brooklyn every day.

After her great pain, though, Rachel could not bring herself to tell Hannah that Arthur had died. We may never know precisely why. Perhaps she felt that Hannah, now in her seventies, might not be able to bear the news and so decided to protect her. Or perhaps Rachel was simply unable to find within herself the words necessary to speak about such a loss.

For whatever reason, Rachel resurrected Arthur and began to speak of him in her letters as she always had. She raised up Arthur like Lazarus, time and again. Had anyone suggested to Rachel that she had plucked Arthur up from the dead against his will, she would have denied it. Every time she brought her son back to life, she would have said, he was glad of it: no chest pain anymore, ever. He could run with his children and fish and worry around the golf course on Saturdays—and he did, with no pain anywhere, only the blessed motions of the spirit.

Rachel did not believe in an afterlife; but she had no trouble inventing one for Arthur. She was now almost eighty years old and her memory for recent events had begun to fail, but she remembered the old days better than ever. So she embellished her memory, but only a little: Arthur's working hard, she wrote, watching his weight; the grandchildren growing like weeds. And things were not as they were, but as Rachel wished them to be.

We do know that Rachel kept hanging on her bedroom wall a favorite picture of Arthur. Nightly she took it down and held it to her breast as she sat in her rocking chair. And there are those who say she talked to that picture every night before she placed it back upon the wall and, thus consoled, went to sleep. Hannah, of course, never knew any of this.

And so the letters passed as regularly as the morning papers and the subway. And Hannah, in Brooklyn, like any good reader miles or centuries away, was a believer. Though she was solicitous of all her sister's children, Arthur, the firstborn, was clearly her favorite. Every year, in March, Hannah sent Arthur a birthday card, but without expecting a reply from him: he was surely too busy. Thus, Hannah entered into Rachel's dream with her whole being. In her letters to Rachel, she often asked for details about

Arthur's life: how the store was doing, the antics of the grandchildren, questions any aunt would have. And she often ended her letters with the phrase "Tell Arthur that I love him." And Rachel did just that. So Rachel embroidered and Hannah wove and the spirit and the face of Arthur did not die. The plot of his life unfolded and burgeoned in the waning years of the two old women's lives. And Hannah followed Rachel's words from the letters to her mind's eye where she could see it all: the picnics, the holidays, the fishing trips, even the size of the bass.

Over the next ten years, Rachel herself gradually grew weak and fragile. Though her mind remained alert, she took to her bed in the big two-story house. A live-in nurse was obtained to help care for her. But a short time later, she had a stroke, lapsed into coma, and died. She would have been ninety the next June. Arthur was still fifty-five.

It fell to Rachel's remaining son to tell Hannah that her sister had died. But that was not his only duty. Cleaning out his mother's desk, he came across his aunt's letters—and learned the truth about all these years. He now had to tell Hannah not only that her sister had died, but that all of her fictions had died with her. It was the most difficult letter he would ever have to write. The words were elusive and slow to come. He thought of the fine line between some fictions and the truth. He even thought momentarily of trying to carry on, a little longer, his mother's tales about Arthur, for Hannah's sake. But in the end, he decided his aunt was entitled to the truth. So he labored and the letter was sent to Dumas Street. There, in the brownstone, two deaths were mourned, rather than only one. And there was, then, no grief like Hannah's in all of Brooklyn.

◈

A Change of Heart

◈

During a recent Parents' Day at the School of Medicine, a surgeon reviewed the major steps involved in transplantation of the heart. The audience, made up primarily of laypersons, was polite and interested. Next, the surgeon introduced, from out of the audience, a vigorous smiling man as someone who'd received a heart transplant only six weeks before. The audience was hushed, rapt as they heard his story. Here was technology made flesh, an ethical dilemma in street clothes, someone with whom, at the coffee break, they could—and did—shake hands.

$\mathcal{T}$he year is 1969, the patient a forty-seven-year-old man with severe heart failure. His surgeons are Dr. Denton Cooley and his team at Houston's Texas Heart Institute. Cardiac surgery is being done to remove extensively scarred and weakened parts of the patient's heart muscle. The surgery goes smoothly enough, but near the end, it becomes clear that the man's heart cannot support his blood pressure. His diseased heart is too weak; in the jargon of the operating room, "he won't come off the pump."

All surgery involves an act of faith. Open-heart surgery is something like a space launch: once the launch has begun, there simply *has* to be enough fuel for the return journey. In this case, there isn't. The patient's chest remains open on the operating table, his life sustained only by the temporary heart–lung machine used during cardiac surgery. A dramatic decision is made, one that Dr. Cooley had known might become necessary at some point: an artificial heart is the only possible answer. First, the patient's sick heart is removed. Then, an artificial heart, designed by Dr. Cooley's team, is inserted. Amazingly, only fifteen minutes after the incision is closed, the patient begins to regain consciousness. His prototype mechanical heart functions perfectly for sixty-four hours; then a donor heart is found and a cardiac transplant is performed.

That patient of Dr. Cooley's, unfortunately, lived only thirty-two hours after the transplant (he died of pneumonia). Still, medical history had been made: an artificial heart had been used in a human, and it had worked.

★　★　★

To replace the human heart with a mechanical pump is an old dream, one through which, over the decades, thousands of scientists have walked. In 1934, Dr. Michael DeBakey designed a "roller pump" in which two rollers "milk" a piece of plastic tubing in one direction, causing blood to flow. Dr. DeBakey's pump was used for rapid transfusion of blood—but its *design* was incorporated into the type of machine most commonly used in heart surgery today. In 1953, Dr. John Gibbon used a "heart–lung" machine (which took over the function of both heart and lungs) to correct an intracardiac defect successfully. In the fifties, too, Dr. Willem Kolff, inventor of the earlier artificial kidney, turned his attention to the mechanical heart; in the sixties, so did Dr. Adrian Kantrowitz. By the seventies, Dr. Robert Jarvik was designing a series of artificial hearts at the University of Utah, to which Dr. Barney Clark came for help in 1982.

There is one particularly fascinating early chapter in the development of the artificial heart. In 1930, three years after his historic nonstop flight from New York to Paris, Charles Lindbergh embarked on another, and little-known, mission. It began when a family member with pneumonia developed "lesions on the heart." Lindbergh asked if such lesions could be removed surgically but was told that surgery on the heart itself was impossible. It occurred to Lindbergh that, with his mechanical aptitude, he might be able to develop a pump that could provide circulation while cardiac surgery was done. Lindbergh was soon introduced to Dr. Alexis Carrel of the Rockefeller Institute. Carrel had been working on a "perfusion pump" that would keep tissues alive for study; his aims thus overlapped with those of Lindbergh, who joined his lab at Rockefeller as a volunteer. Despite Lindbergh's fame, he was able to work effectively, and he supervised the construction of dozens of pumps between 1930 and 1938. The pumps could, indeed, sustain life. For example, a kidney hooked to it shortly began to put out urine. Journalists dubbed the pump a "robot heart"; and it was exhibited at the 1939 World's Fair. But the promising work of this unlikely pair was halted by World War II.

Consider flight as an analogy. The Wright brothers' flight at Kitty Hawk in 1903 lasted twelve seconds; by 1905, their plane stayed up for thirty-eight minutes. In a similar way, in 1957, artificial hearts implanted in animals could support life for only ninety minutes. But by 1979, an artificial heart, the Jarvik-7, had sustained life in a calf for more than seven months. By 1979, too, though he had no way of knowing it, Dr. Barney Clark, a Seattle dentist, was moving toward his own historic encounter with the Jarvik-7.

Dr. Clark's saga, with elements of heroism and tragedy, brings to mind another famous flight, that of the mythological figure Icarus. Icarus escaped imprisonment in the Labyrinth by flying on wings of feathers held together with wax; but he flew too near the sun, the wax melted, and he fell into the sea and drowned. Dr. Clark's flight was to last 112 turbulent days before he, too, perished.

Barney Clark had been a handsome, vigorous man. But by late 1982, he was terminally ill. His cardiac problem was heart muscle disease of unknown cause (still today the most common reason for transplantation). His heart was pumping very feebly, only 20 percent of normal; his lungs, abdomen, and legs were congested, his breathing labored. All medical therapy had failed.

Earlier in 1982, Dr. Clark had met with the cardiology staff at the University of Utah, including the cardiac surgeon Dr. William DeVries. Dr. Clark was shown the laboratories where the Jarvik hearts were made. He came to understand that the artificial heart was an experimental device. But both he and his physicians hoped that it might extend his life—and improve its quality.

Others had volunteered to receive the first "permanent" artificial heart. Several convicts on death row, for example, had asked to be the first recipients of the device, noting that the machine could simply be stopped when time for their execution arrived. Though these offers were turned down, they underscore the complex ethical issues surrounding this new technology.

Dr. Clark's surgery was done by Dr. DeVries and his team on December 1, 1982, a day earlier than originally intended: it was feared that Clark might not survive an additional twenty-four hours. The surgery took about eight hours. After Dr. Clark's diseased heart was removed, the Jarvik-7 heart was placed. The Jarvik heart, like that used by Dr. Cooley in 1969, was powered by compressed air. The air, pumped through tubes in the patient's chest into the device, caused movements of a "diaphragm," which propelled the blood through the substitute heart; the pump filled from Dr. Clark's veins and emptied into his arteries via artificial valves.

The next sixteen weeks, made up of triumphs and tragedy, were witnessed by the whole world. Dr. Clark remained tethered, like an astronaut, by the lines of his pump. Though he was never able to leave the hospital, he often appeared to be of heroic good cheer. In a television interview, he expressed the opinion that "All in all, it's been a pleasure to be able to help people." He believed firmly that he and his wife were "co-investigators" with the Utah research team. Despite his bravery, though, Dr. Clark must have undergone a great deal of suffering, both emotional and physical. His course after surgery was complicated by mental confusion; seizures; valve dysfunction (which required more surgery); severe nosebleeds (made worse by medicine used to prevent clots in the machine); and, finally, by failure of several organs, notably the kidneys. Still, the artificial heart provided Barney Clark with 12,912,499 beats. Like Icarus, he has entered our mythology, on imperfect wings to be sure, but for more than a while, flying.

A few days after insertion of his artificial heart in late 1982, Dr. Barney Clark sat up on the side of his bed, dangled his legs, joked with nurses, and listened to a recording of Handel's *Messiah*. His wife wondered whimsically whether he might no longer love his family, since he didn't have his old heart. That afternoon I received a phone call asking for my comments on the heart as the "seat of the emotions." During our chat, I mused about the Tin Man in *The Wizard of Oz,* who sang "If I Only Had a Heart." The Wizard granted his wish, in the form of a cutout heart. The artificial heart, unfortunately, is more complex than that, grounded less in magic than in the painstaking work of thousands of researchers over many decades.

Since Dr. Clark's death, clinical experience with the total artificial heart has continued to be disappointing—and sobering. In 1984 and 1985, Dr. DeVries inserted the heart in three more patients: two survived a year but had major complications; the third patient lived only ten days.

One other approach that has paralleled development of the total artificial heart deserves mention. This approach aims at boosting the function of the left ventricle (the heart's main pumping chamber) with pumps called Left Ventricular Assist Devices (LVADs). Some of these units are as small as an adult fist, which allows their insertion, for example, below the muscle layer of the abdominal wall. The device functions *in parallel* with the patient's failing heart, which remains in place. The pump fills from the patient's heart, then expels that blood into the arteries, improving the circulation. One advantage of such a device is that the patient's own heart can serve as a "backup" should the device fail. LVADs could ultimately play a role in the care of more than one hundred thousand patients a year. Their main role at present is as a short-term bridge to cardiac transplantation: some 20 percent of patients awaiting transplant die before a donor heart is found. But others might benefit from LVADs, too: those with postoperative heart failure (as in Dr. Cooley's 1969 case) and those with temporary heart failure after a heart attack.

Is there a workable total artificial heart on the horizon?

Perhaps not immediately, but there may be in the future. I'll be surprised if we don't continue to try to develop one. The clinical need, after all, is great: thousands could benefit annually from such a device—and the number of hearts available for transplantation seems likely to remain far too limited to meet the demand. The recent promising experience with LVADs gives me reason for modest optimism about the total artificial heart. Perhaps we ought to take a lesson from the work of Dr. Willem Kolff—his artificial *kidney* was abysmally unsuccessful in early trials. Today it offers hope—and life—to thousands every year.

Heart Transplants

Dr. Norman Shumway of Stanford University recently labeled the 1980s "the decade of heart transplantation." It was Dr. Shumway who, in 1960, with Dr. Richard Lower, perfected the basic transplant operation in use today.

However, it was Dr. Christiaan Barnard of the University of Cape Town, South Africa, who did the first two human transplants in the world. The first patient, Louis Washkansky, received the heart of a twenty-five-year-old woman on December 2, 1967. The patient lived only eighteen days, dying of pneumonia, an infection undoubtedly made difficult to treat because of the drugs used to minimize the body's rejection of the heart.

Dr. Shumway performed the first human transplant in the United States in January 1968. One of those early patients, Willem Van Buren, received his heart more than nineteen years ago and is the longest-living survivor—it's conjectured that the tissue "match" in Van Buren's case happened to be extremely good, resulting in less rejection. But his case was unusual; in those early years of cardiac transplantation, only 20 percent of the patients survived even one year.

The major advance in cardiac transplantation has been in

preventing rejection of the heart. One antirejection medication, cyclosporine, made widely available in 1983, deserves much of the credit for current survival statistics in transplant patients: nearly 90 percent survival during the first two years after surgery, about 75 percent survival after five years.

In 1973, only 22 heart transplants were done in the United States. In 1988, there were 1,630. But an estimated fourteen thousand to fifteen thousand patients who could benefit from transplantation die each year in this country. In part, this is because the maximum number of donor hearts available is limited, perhaps two thousand a year. This mismatch leads to ethical questions having to do with utilization, distribution, and rationing of scarce medical resources and with health-care financing. Some voices urge that funding for expensive procedures such as transplantation should be diverted instead into improved efforts at preventive medicine. Most patients who receive heart transplants, however, have primary heart muscle disease; preventive medicine has little to offer for this type of heart disease. One point is clear: Research in artificial hearts and transplants must go hand in hand. At this point in the cardiac story, both are needed.

My surgical colleagues assure me that cardiac transplant operations are not technically difficult when compared to other types of cardiac surgery. First, the patient is placed on heart–lung bypass, the machine that provides blood and oxygen to vital organs during the surgery. Then the diseased heart is removed. At this point, there are only four connections to be made in inserting the donor heart. First, the two atria of the donor heart are sewn to the remnants of the recipient's own atria—this allows the "inflow" vessels of the heart (veins from the body and from the lungs) to work properly. Then, the "outflow" vessels, the aorta (to the body) and the pulmonary artery (to the lungs), are joined within the recipient's chest. Finally, the patient is weaned from the heart–lung machine: if all goes as expected, he and his new heart are on their own.

If the transplant operation is a relatively simple one for the surgeon, it does not seem so to the patient. It is more like a miracle, restoring to him the vision of himself before he sickened unto death. He has taken this foreign body, this heart, into himself, like an amoeba, but with more difficulty, and out of greater need. Sylvia Plath wrote, "Love set you going like a fat gold watch." Having a new heart must feel something like that; and love *is* involved. The gift-heart is now part of the patient's machinery. A philosopher would pronounce it both necessary and sufficient.

In every heart transplant operation, there is one moment that is especially provocative for me. It is the moment when the recipient's diseased heart has been removed, still feebly beating, and placed in a salt solution for pathological study. The patient is on the heart-lung machine, but the donor heart has not yet been sewn in place. The "heart nest" is, for the moment, completely empty. Are the human emotions we locate in the heart, temporarily at least, in abeyance?

Mr. Simmons can't answer that question, of course: he was asleep at the time. Mr. Simmons is a tall, balding man, forty-nine years old, owner of a small business in middle Georgia. Four months ago, following a series of heart attacks that caused major damage to his own heart, he received a heart transplant. This morning, he is cheerful and talkative. He is here for another in a series of heart biopsies. A heart biopsy is the only procedure in medicine in which the surgeon is not concerned with stopping any bleeding he may have caused. In biopsy of the lining of the heart, any bleeding, of course, leaks directly back into the patient's bloodstream.

Mr. Simmons stretches out comfortably on the table; as he does so he points out to us that now he can sleep flat in his bed at home. While waiting for his transplant (a full three weeks in the hospital), he was so short of breath that he had to sleep bolt upright every night—his lungs were that congested.

Heart biopsy is necessary in order to detect the earliest signs of rejection of his new heart. The technique—taking a small piece of the heart for examination under the microscope—sounds daunting but is now rather routine. It takes less than thirty minutes and causes the patient little discomfort (in part because the nerves of the transplanted heart have been disrupted by the surgery).

Under local anesthesia, the surgeon enters the circulation through a neck vein. No incision in the vein is required, only a needle stick (Mr. Simmons says that this is the only part that hurts, but the discomfort is only momentary). The special biopsy catheter, twenty inches long and a bit thicker than a pencil lead, is threaded into the neck vein and follows, with minimal guidance, the blood back to the heart. After the tip of the catheter has been positioned within the heart, small cutting jaws at the tip of the catheter open, then close, snipping off a tiny piece of heart muscle. This specimen is then whisked off to the pathology lab for examination. The microscopic sections will dictate any adjustments in the medicines Mr. Simmons takes to prevent rejection of his heart transplant.

As he dresses, Mr. Simmons tells me that his chest is now minimally sore, only a twinge now and then. He's driving his car again (driving was interdicted until the two halves of his breastbone, wired together at surgery, knitted securely). He's working every day, walking ten miles a week, and aiming at twenty.

It is one thing to discuss, in the abstract, the fiscal, societal, and ethical dilemmas posed by the technology of heart transplantation. It's another matter to feel the pulse of a patient who has received a heart—or to lose a patient who might have benefited. Here is the pedagogic word made flesh; the first dimension, the human one.

As he leaves the hospital on his way back home, Mr. Simmons is smiling broadly. And well he might be. Four months ago, he was at death's literal door. Today, he is the lost son whose return is celebrated; and witness to the small recurring miracle of systole. The steady reassuring thump within his chest may not yet be wholly his own; but by now, it's beginning to have the feel of family about it. And the scroll of his life, his *tabula rasa,* which had been about to stop unrolling, seems now to have some white space left on which to write.

Breath

The first breath of an infant is more than simply an initial gulp from our ocean of air. In that instant, as the newborn passes from the marine to the mundane, a number of wondrous changes take place in its circulation. With first inspiration, the lungs uncoil like flowers in time-lapse photography; as this happens the arteries of the lungs, crimped and cramped during fetal life, expand to their first full flow of blood, wakening to work. The fetal vessel that served to "bypass" the lungs during uterine life begins to close on its own, its mission accomplished (if it *fails* to close, a condition known as "patent ductus arteriosus" ensues and sometimes requires cardiac surgery). All these changes relate to that first fateful breath that no one remembers. Some subsequent breaths, as it happens, may be just as full of portent.

Sometimes, in the rush, flash, and beep, the slow accordion of traffic, it has seemed to me that the whole world is hyperventilating—all five billion of us, sentenced to oxygen for life, overbreathing as one, and sharing the feeling that we'd be fine if only we could get in that one good deep breath.

But breathing is supposed to be automatic and unconscious, like the tide that it is. It's precisely when we *think* about our breathing that we get into trouble. Abnormal respiratory patterns are common; virtually everyone has experienced hyperventilation, for example. Other breathing patterns can be dramatic, even diagnostic: take the case of Mr. Alexander.

I saw him first in 1975, when he was seventy-two years old, a retired clergyman, a Michigander come south to visit his daughter. He had clear-cut heart disease, his loud murmurs the result of rheumatic fever in his youth. Mild heart failure two years earlier had responded to medicines, but it was evident that, in time, he would need cardiac surgery: at least one heart valve needed to be replaced. After I told him my opinion, he smiled broadly and graciously, then declined, saying that "something else will wear out before my heart does!" I understood his reluctance; he *was* getting along pretty well. I saw Mr. Alexander from time to time when he visited his daughter—and letters went back and forth between us. He was an inveterate reader of *The Merck Manual*; he deciphered my reports about his condition in the light of that venerable medical reference book, calling it "surefire," but "direful reading at best!" As his symptoms worsened over the next four Michigan winters, he gave up the book as being "too luridly realistic for good bedside reading." He went on, "I am thinking of substituting something by Norman Vincent Peale." By virtue of his extracurricular reading, he knew that he was slipping back into heart failure; but he didn't want me to know.

One April evening in 1979, Mr. Alexander called me at home to announce that he was again in town for a visit. As we talked I noticed that his breathing over the phone was quite noisy and close to my ear, loud enough to mar the usual ministerial resonance of his voice. Then, a few seconds later, I couldn't hear his breathing at all. My God, I said to myself, this man has Cheyne–Stokes respirations! Sure enough, as our chat continued, back came the noisy rasp of his breathing, then fifteen to twenty seconds of absolute silence, waxing and waning in cycles.

This breathing pattern suggests severe heart failure; I offered to see him at once, that evening. He declined, politely, saying that he and his daughter were on their way to hear a performance of the Metropolitan Opera on its annual southern tour. In desperation, I asked that he take an extra "water pill" and meet me at my office early the next day. The following morning, he assured me that he'd enjoyed *Tannhäuser,* though he'd had to make a considerable number of rest stops during the performance: the diuretic had worked. His Cheyne–Stokes respirations, still present, were less florid. I'd already arranged for a hospital bed. Shortly thereafter, he had open-heart surgery, with replacement of his diseased aortic valve (with a "porcine" valve, harvested from a pig). Within a few days, Mr. Alexander was breathing normally, if painfully, post-op. He's now eighty-five, still regaling me with his wit and wisdom and, occasionally, a puckish quote from *Merck*. He does ask me, now and again, just how long the life span of a pig is.

Normal respiration takes place as a result of messages sent out from the medulla, the lower part of the brain, situated just above the spinal cord. The medulla works in coordination with several other brain areas involved with breathing. Right and left phrenic nerves carry these messages through the chest cavity, ending at the diaphragm, the broad flat muscle that separates the abdomen and chest. Descent of the diaphragm renders the chest cavity more "negative" in its pressure and initiates *in*spiration. *Ex*piration is usually a more passive act brought about by the inward collapse of the elastic chest cage and its muscles. Regulation of normal respiration is accomplished by monitoring of the blood by special "chemoreceptor" areas located both in the medulla and in the walls of the carotid arteries in the neck. These receptors respond to changing levels of oxygen, carbon dioxide, and acidity. Thus, the uptake of oxygen and the release of carbon dioxide by the lungs, the raison d'être of breathing, is regulated with minute-to-minute meticulous care.

Cheyne–Stokes respirations were first described by two nineteenth-century physicians. In heart failure, the pattern may result because the "transit time" of blood between heart and brain is prolonged, delaying arrival of the usual signals at the medulla. The brain thus responds to a message that *was* true but has been rendered false by the circulatory delay. The regulatory system, thrown out of sync, cycles futilely, always responding too late, like a dog chasing its tail.

Though breathing is usually automatic, when necessary we can assert *voluntary* control over it: we can hold our breath, breathe faster or slower, deeply or less deeply, as our exercise level or emotion demands. And we can cry, gasp, sigh, groan, laugh, and talk, all acts that involve the respiratory apparatus. These voluntary uses of breathing are integrated in complex ways by involvement of the cerebral cortex and other higher brain centers. Nevertheless, these higher centers are not essential for maintenance of normal rhythmic breathing. This is why a person who is pronounced "brain-dead" (after head injury, for example) can continue to breathe for months or even years: The lower medullary centers are still intact.

A dramatic example of breathing gone awry is the plight of those who stop breathing while they sleep, a syndrome known as "sleep apnea." Most sleep apnea is due to intermittent upper airway obstruction. Its victims are most often obese males, some of whom are called "Pickwickian," after Dickens's rotund and sleepy character Joe. During deep sleep, the tongue of such a patient falls backward, obstructing the airway. The result can be a dangerous fall in the blood oxygen level (and a rise in carbon dioxide); other findings may include loud snoring; struggling efforts to breathe; uncontrollable, violent movements of the limbs; bed-wetting; cardiac rhythm problems, heart attacks, even death. Such patients have excessive daytime sleepiness and often combat an irresistible urge to sleep; because they cannot stay awake, many have automobile accidents or lose their jobs. Most patients with sleep apnea show signs of "sleep deprivation"—intellectual deterioration and changes in personality, such as anxiety, irritability, and depression.

"Ondine's curse" is another cause of sleep apnea. Ondine was one of Neptune's many children, a water nymph who fell in love with a mortal. He had the poor judgment to jilt Ondine, whereupon he received one of the most diabolical judgments ever meted out: Ondine took away from him all automatic functions, which required that he remember to breathe. Thus, to fall asleep, to forget to breathe, was to die, which was his exact fate. In the medical counterpart of this Greek myth, Ondine's curse, automatic control of breathing is impaired, but voluntary control remains intact. The problem in these patients is not "obstructive" but "central"—they do not struggle to breathe when sleeping but simply stop breathing, presumably as a result of incompletely understood changes in the brain's respiratory centers.

Treatment of patients with sleep apnea must be prescribed individually. In obstructive apnea, weight loss, though difficult to accomplish and to sustain, may help. Use of a tracheostomy (a surgical opening in the windpipe) at night can "bypass" the obstructing tongue and give significant relief. Surgery for enlarged tonsils or nasal obstruction may benefit some patients. In patients with Ondine's curse, surgically placed "pacemakers" may be used to stimulate the diaphragm at night (one side at a time, to prevent fatigue of the nerve); the drug progesterone and ventilation devices may help as well.

Compared to the potentially lethal abnormalities that we have been discussing, hyperventilation may seem like a minor problem. Yet this syndrome is infinitely more common than Cheyne–Stokes respirations and sleep apnea; and it can be incapacitating. Hyperventilation, as the name implies, means "overbreathing." Hyperventilation is both expected and desirable in many states—in pneumonia, for example, or during exercise. Most commonly when we speak of hyperventilation, however, we are referring to the *overbreathing that accompanies anxiety*; early cases were seen in soldiers during battle. Overbreathing results in a lowering of the blood carbon dioxide, and it is this chemical imbalance that causes the symptoms. Most often, the patient has the feeling that he "can't get in a good deep breath"—in fact, the problem is precisely that he's *already* taken in too many "good deep breaths." Other symptoms include frequent deep "sighing" respirations, light-headedness, a sense of suffocation, tingling around the mouth and the tips of the fingers, and various kinds of chest pain (from "stabbing" or "sharp" to "dull" or "aching"). Simply being aware of one's breathing for a time can bring on symptoms of hyperventilation: I found myself hyperventilating, for example, while reading and writing about Ondine's curse! A simple explanation of the problem often helps a patient with hyperventilation understand that his symptoms are due to his having interfered, unwittingly, with a mechanism that's supposed to be on "automatic."

Mark Twain's comment is appropriate here: "Each person is born to one possession which outvalues all his others—his last breath." In their professional duties, physicians are called upon to "pronounce" many patients, to append to a life the precise time and details of its ending. For me, such a ceremony has always had an eerie feel about it, standing there at the bedside, watching for the least sign of life. Especially as an intern, one wants to be "sure" about such a matter, not to say "Yes, he's gone" prematurely, to give the patient the benefit of one's witness. But of the times I've been summoned to bedsides in order to pronounce in such matters, one stands out in my memory.

Several years ago, late at night, the doorbell rang at my house. At the door was the woman from the house across the street. She was clearly distraught. "Please come quickly," she said. "I think he's dying." I went with her in the darkness.

On the way, I turned over in my mind what I knew of her husband's medical problems: mainly that he was in his late seventies and fragile with severe angina. In the past I'd seen him out walking his dog, but very slowly, lest he incur the wrath of his heart. As his wife and I hurried across the lawn, she interrupted my thoughts with "He was lying there on his recliner. We'd had a nice evening. He put down the book he'd been reading without saying a word. Then his breathing changed—became slow, noisy. He didn't answer me when I spoke to him. So I came to get you as fast as I could."

"I'm glad you did," I said as we entered the hall. I asked her to wait there and made my way back to the den.

He was completely motionless on the recliner until I approached him. Then he took a shallow breath, which startled me. I waited for a minute or so, but he didn't breathe again. I had no stethoscope with me. I opened his shirt and placed my ear on his chest. Nothing. As I listened, though, he took in another breath, or tried to. That was his last. I waited several minutes more. There was nothing. His color was the purple color of death, which comes just as the ghost leaves us. I went back to the hall and told his wife, "I'm sorry. He's gone." I put my arm around her. She offered to make me some coffee and, though I didn't want to stay awake, I let her. I called the ambulance for her, called some relatives to come stay with her. I said good night. On the way home in the darkness, I realized that Emily Dickinson had foretold all this in one of her poems, the one that begins, "There's Been a Death in the Opposite House." In some ways, it may seem strange that I'd think of a poem at a time like that. But writers make a life out of such lines. And so do some cardiologists.

A Family Matter

Except for the literature of popular psychology, the word *syndrome* is not that commonly used outside medicine. But the word is a useful one and its etymology helps explain its meaning. *Syndrome* comes from the Greek *syn,* "with," plus *dramein,* "to run." A syndrome is a *collection of symptoms or signs* that "run with" each other. Frequently in medicine, it's not one particular finding that is the absolute clue to a diagnosis, but a combination of findings: for example, a skin rash *plus* a heart murmur *plus* fatigue, all together, may suggest endocarditis, an infection of the lining of the heart. The concept of a syndrome, of findings occurring together, also helps a physician in the diagnosis of "new" diseases, even when the underlying *cause* of such disease is not clear—in other words, when we're still pretty ignorant.

She is here at the cardiac clinic with her two children. I am scheduled to check the hearts of both, a boy and a girl. They are slender grade-schoolers, tall for their ages, well behaved. Their mother is pleasant, well groomed, also tall, about thirty years old. She wears glasses that, I note as we chat, have thick lenses. It's summer and she's wearing a red T-shirt. Ordinarily, I'd reflexly read the wry message on her shirt. But my gaze stops instead at the sagging neck of her shirt—she's telling me about her children's early years, but I'm distracted—peeping just above her shirt is an unmistakable clue that the cardiac surgeon has preceded me in talking with her. There is a fine, well-healed surgical scar that clearly extends downward, through the middle of her breastbone. At some point in the past she's had cardiac surgery herself. I put this fact together with the thick lenses of her glasses, the thin limbs of her children, and I know, all at once, even before she tells me, the reason she's here: I'm to examine her children to see if they have Marfan's syndrome.

In 1896, Antonin Marfan, a professor of pediatrics in Paris, described some features of the condition that bears his name. His patient was a five-and-a-half-year-old girl, Gabrielle. She was thin, with long limbs, and especially long fingers, which Marfan likened to the legs of a spider. The medical term for this finding, "arachnodactyly," derives from the name Arachne, the peasant girl of mythology; the goddess Minerva changed her into a spider because the quality of her weaving rivaled her own. Since Marfan's original description, stressing these skeletal findings, we have learned that people with Marfan's may have problems in several other systems, notably the eye and the heart.

I take a brief history from the mother. Yes, she tells me, she does have Marfan's—and she has had cardiac surgery, several years ago. Before she goes on with her story, I ask if I may examine her eyes briefly with a flashlight. She nods: she's often been a patient at the major teaching hospital in which I work. I turn the light toward her eyes. As I do, suddenly, in memory, I am twenty-five years younger, in this same clinic, examining the eyes of a young boy with Marfan's. I am reminded now of that exam because, during it, I made a vivid personal discovery.

That afternoon, years ago, my patient was a young boy, maybe ten years old. Stretched out full-length on the table, he, like the children I am to see today, was thin and tall. He had other skeletal problems, as well: there was a deep vertical furrow in his breastbone; and he had a mild curvature of the spine. I examined his heart; a murmur pointed to a leak of one of the valves. I asked him to sit up so I could examine his eyes.

Twenty-five years ago, I felt I was getting pretty good at examining hearts. But I was on much shakier ground in terms of the eye. Oh, I could see the retina (at the back of the eye) easily enough, the vessels there splaying out around the moon-colored optic nerve that ferries signals from the eye back to the brain. Still, I was far from expert at knowing what to look for, specifically, in the eyes of a patient with suspected Marfan's. What happened then was happenstance.

I was simply checking whether the boy's pupils constricted, as they normally should, in response to a bright light. I shone my light at his eye; as I did he averted his gaze. When his eyes shifted, my light shone tangentially on his iris, the colored part of the eye. To my surprise, the mottled blue of his iris trembled and fluttered momentarily, like a flag in a breeze. Startled, I asked the boy to move his eyes from side to side a few times; I'd never seen this before. After clinic, I lit out for the medical library to find out just what this curious "sign of the tremulous iris" might have to do with Marfan's syndrome. Soon thereafter, I was busy at work on my first medical paper, which pointed out to cardiologists that this simple physical finding, the tremor of the iris—"iridodonesis" is the medical term—could be helpful to them in terms of detection of Marfan's syndrome. (My findings, of course, were not new under the sun: iridodonesis is well known in the work of an ophthalmologist; it simply took us heart doctors a while to get the word.)

Ironically, it appears now that Gabrielle, Marfan's first patient, may not have been an example of the syndrome as we view it today. An ophthalmologist in Cincinnati may deserve the honor of having been the first (some twenty years before Marfan) to describe the cluster of features that has come to be known as Marfan's: he described displaced lenses of the eyes ("ectopia lentis") in a brother and sister who also had long limbs and overly "mobile" joints. Such are the vagaries of medical history, at times, that one person sows but another reaps.

I come back to the present and the mother: under my light, her irises tremble like chandeliers. I take a brief history from her, but I'm thinking all the while about her two children, still waiting patiently. My examination of them, its *yes* or *no*, is likely to be a very important moment in their young lives.

The central abnormality that links the disparate problems (skeleton, eye, and heart) that may occur in Marfan's syndrome is an inborn disorder of the body's connective tissue, the "glue" that holds together and supports other tissues. Patients with the condition often announce themselves to the physician because of the *skeletal* features: they are often (but not always) unusually tall and slender, with long extremities, and a body shape that can be quite similar to that of a basketball player. Other bony abnormalities may include curvature of the spine; the breastbone may be either protuberant or sunken. Finally, there is a tendency toward lax or excessively mobile joints. (Many patients, for example, can bend the thumb back along the wrist until it touches the forearm—I hasten to add that some "normal" people can also do this, especially women, who tend to be more loose-jointed than men.)

For years, it's been theorized that several famous historical figures may have had Marfan's syndrome. The lanky stature and long fingers of Abraham Lincoln drew attention to the possibility that he had the condition. It's been conjectured that two composers, Franz Liszt, the virtuosic pianist, and the fiery Italian violinist Niccolò Paganini, may have had Marfan's. The great majority of basketball players, despite their body shapes, do *not* have Marfan's—but a few do, and the result, if the syndrome goes undetected, can be tragic, as we shall see.

In the eye of a patient with Marfan's syndrome, the lens may be dislocated from its usual place, centered behind the iris; this occurs because the tiny ligaments that fix the lens in place are disrupted (another manifestation of the faulty connective tissue). The tremor of the iris that I saw twenty-five years ago (and have just seen in the mother of my two new patients) is related to the fact that the lens normally supports the iris, restricting its movement. But when the lens is dislocated, the iris may flutter. (This flutter is only a rough sign; a complete exam of the eye requires use of a special instrument called a "slit lamp.")

The heart of the matter in Marfan's syndrome is the *heart* itself. First, the heart valves, which keep blood flowing in the proper direction within the heart, have a tendency to leak; such leaks cause heart murmurs and can increase the work load of the heart. Most importantly, the aorta, the largest artery, has a tendency to enlarge and develop weak spots—aneurysms—which, under stress, can rupture, leading to sudden death.

Over the past few years, the deaths of several excellent athletes, including some outstanding basketball players, have focused national attention on Marfan's syndrome. Perhaps the best known of these athletes was Flo Hyman, the six-foot-five-inch Olympic volleyball star who died suddenly, on tour, at the age of thirty-one, of a ruptured aorta; an autopsy confirmed the diagnosis of Marfan's, previously unsuspected, in this superb athlete.

An estimated 25,000 to 30,000 people in the United States have Marfan's syndrome. The familial association may be striking: in one family in Kentucky, 93 family members, out of a total of 219, were affected over 6 generations. Though Marfan's usually comes to the attention of medicine slowly, one case at a time, its genealogic footprints can often be seen when the physician can get a complete family history. If one parent has the syndrome, statistically *half* of his or her children will be affected. The sex incidence is equal and all ethnic groups may be affected. In 25 percent to 30 percent of cases, however, there is no family history to suggest Marfan's: these cases seem to occur because of a sporadic—and unpredictable—mutation in one of the parent's genes (statistically, such mutations seem to correlate with the father's being older than average).

But the genetics of Marfan's is often not simple. For one thing, even if the culprit gene is inherited by a child, the *expression* of that gene may be variable—which means that patients may differ dramatically from one another. For example, some may have arachnodactyly with only a slightly enlarged aorta; in others, the gene may express itself more dangerously in the form of an aneurysm, as in Flo Hyman's case.

The mother tells me now about her surgery. There is always, for me, a sense of the heroic about patients who have had cardiac surgery. That sense has doubtless been reinforced, in my case, by the fact that I make it a point to visit the operating room when one of my patients has cardiac surgery. It is one thing to listen to a heart and its murmurs—and something else to see that heart at surgery, inert and murmurless, the squeeze-box temporarily tuneless.

The mother's surgery was quite typical for the aortic problems seen in Marfan's patients. After she was placed on the heart–lung machine, which supports life during the operation, the weakened and widened first part of her aorta (just as it leaves the heart) was removed, together with the leaking aortic valve that leads to it. Then a composite graft was sewn in. In a composite graft, an artificial valve has already been sewn into the Dacron tube that will replace the diseased portion of the aorta. Insertion of such a composite graft, a relatively recent innovation, has shortened operative time and reduced the risk of surgery in patients with Marfan's. At the end of such surgery, an electrical shock is applied to the stunned heart, which immediately revs up: the genie is once more back in the bottle.

Dramatic improvements in the care of such patients have also occurred outside the surgical arena. Echocardiography (cardiac ultrasound) and magnetic resonance imaging are both helpful in following patients with Marfan's. Both techniques are noninvasive: no pain is involved, an important factor in the care of young patients. And both are sensitive in assessment of aortic size and valve leaks. Medications called *beta blockers* are used to lower both the heart rate and the force of contraction of the heart. The aim is to reduce the ordinary daily stresses on the weakened aorta, thereby retarding its enlargement and widening. The mother has been on beta blockers for several years. There is an interesting story behind such medical therapy, one that began not with humans but with turkeys.

Veterinarians have long known that turkeys may develop—and die from—an enlarging aorta similar to that seen in patients with Marfan's. In searching for a treatment, astute researchers found that adding reserpine to the turkey feed (the drug reduces blood pressure and has some actions similar to the newer beta blockers) helped prevent aortic aneurysms and death. It was a short step for cardiologists to realize that such an innovative medical approach might also work in humans with similar problems.

As the mother finishes her story I take out my stethoscope and place it on her chest. Even through her red T-shirt, her heart sounds are crisp and regular. "Sounds good," I say, and she smiles. Our mutual hope is that her surgery has markedly reduced the likelihood that she will experience cataclysmic problems such as those that Flo Hyman suffered. I should mention, in this regard, that after Flo Hyman's death, her brother was examined and Marfan's was diagnosed. Subsequently, like this mother, he also underwent prophylactic aortic surgery.

I turn my attention now to the two children, looking for evidence of Marfan's. I don't have to look far. Both have unmistakable iridodonesis. And each has a heart murmur, not loud, but not normal either. Both have Marfan's. I tell the mother. She had suspected as much. And, of course, she already has firsthand knowledge of what this means. Both children, like their mother, will need to be followed by several specialists. They will need, for example, periodic measurements of their aortic size and monitoring of any eye findings. Most importantly, both these children, like their mother, will have to learn to be fighters. But many people are poised to help them: nurses, social workers, medical and surgical specialists, and, importantly, schoolteachers. Since 1981, the National Marfan Foundation has served as a central clearinghouse for information and support of patients, families, and research on the condition. Every year there is reason for more optimism in both medical and surgical care of these patients. The way ahead for these two will not be easy. But it will be safer than ever before.

◈

Missed Signals:
The Pacemaker Story

◈

Not long ago, I received, as a gift, a tape of marches by John Philip Sousa. Playing it in my car transported me back instantly to high school and college, during which I played clarinet in two superb bands. Memories of those years are even more vivid because the clarinet section marched right behind the majorettes. But when a marching cadence enters the central nervous system, it lays down pathways that are even more indelible than the majorettes. Recently, then, stopped for red lights, I began to draw curious stares from people in the cars around me. Here was this bearded fellow, waiting for the green, his shoulders dipping alternately, torso twisting rhythmically, as though he were marching in place. It's axiomatic, I suppose, that a cardiologist would like Sousa. The heart is always marching, unless it misses signals from its conductor.

$\mathcal{M}$edical students memorize more than facts: along the way, they also commit many patients to memory. Mr. Trammell was such a patient for me in 1962, when I was a senior student. His problem was an intermittent—and dangerous—slowing of his heart rate. Though usually steady at 70 to 100 beats a minute, periodically his heart rate would plummet, with no warning at all, to 25 beats a minute. When this happened, he fainted, dropping heavily to the ground, often injuring himself in the process. Mr. Trammell told me his story while lying in his hospital bed; wires led from two conducting pads on his chest to a large metal box nearby—the electrical source. Mr. Trammell was relatively serene when I first met him, but he didn't stay serene for long. When his heart rate fell below a set value—say 60 beats a minute—this primitive *external* pacemaker was triggered to fire—and it did. Unfortunately, the electrical stimulus had to be large, intense enough to penetrate the skin and muscles of the chest wall and reach his heart. Thus, each shock of the pacemaker caused pain. Mr. Trammell's rhythmic "Oh! Oh! Oh!" at a paced rate of 60 could be heard up and down the hall until his own capricious heart mercifully took back over. It was several days before a "permanent," though still crude, *internal* pacemaker, flown in to the medical center, could be surgically installed, to the great relief of Mr. Trammell—and his doctors.

The external pacemaker used on Mr. Trammell, hurtful

as it was, was lifesaving—and rather new—technology: the first pacemaker had been implanted by Ake Senning only a few years before. (Its duration of action was quite short, from hours to days. The first successful long-term implantation of a self-contained pacemaker was carried out by Dr. William Chardack and colleagues in Buffalo in June 1960.) But before the pacemaker was possible, scientists first had to understand the heart's own remarkable electrical apparatus, the one we're all born with.

In the embryo, the primitive human heart warms up like an orchestra before the concert. In its earliest form, the heart is a simple tube that becomes a four-chambered structure by an elaborate series of twists, folds, and partitions. But even this earliest "heart-tube" has a mysterious intrinsic beat, a natural inborn rhythm that in this early stage is slow and ponderous (like the bass section, perhaps). As the heart develops, control of the beat passes from one section to another, gradually picking up speed. Thus, early on, the slower-beating ventricle sets the pace, but control is soon usurped by the faster atria. Finally, in the embryo, a small part of the heart at the top of the right atrium—the sinus node—steps to the podium. Its inherent beat is the fastest of any part of the heart and it now assumes the role of permanent conductor of the cardiac orchestra.

The sinus node initiates the electrical activity of the heart, sending it along "wires," or conducting fibers, to the other main battery of the heart, the A-V (atrioventricular) node. Located, as its name implies, between the (upper) atria and (lower) ventricles, the A-V node relays the beat to the rest of the heart, ensuring coordination. Thus, the A-V node can be thought of as concertmaster, carrying out the tempo instructions dictated by the sinus node, whether fast or slow. From the A-V node, the signal passes along special fast-conducting fibers, until it reaches the heart muscle, prompting it to contract. As in Mr. Trammell's case, dysfunction along this circuit—sinus node, A-V node, or the more distant fiber pathways—may require insertion of a cardiac pacemaker.

Our understanding of the electrical apparatus of the heart came slowly. For decades, it was thought that electrical activity originated in ordinary heart muscle. Then a series of interwoven discoveries, like the tangled threads on the back of a tapestry, led to the true picture on the front. In an anatomical sense, discovery of the electrical apparatus occurred in reverse order: the distant specialized conduction system, the "wires," were described in the first half of the 1800s. S. Tawara, a Japanese anatomist working in Germany, described the A-V node in 1906. Finally, in 1907, a young postgraduate medical student, Martin Flack, working at London Hospital (with his mentor, Arthur Keith), saw, under the microscope, a strange structure embedded shallowly in the atrial muscle. He had seen it before but failed to recognize its significance. That day, though, as a squirrel's nest may be recognized only after the oak leaves are dropped, Flack saw the structure for what it was, the master battery of the heart, the sinus node.

Early pacemakers, such as the one used on Mr. Trammell, were primitive. Their relatively simple (and bulky) electronic circuitry could usually be depended on to pulse at a preset rate (about 70 in the adult). But batteries lasted only eighteen months or less, then had to be replaced (under local anesthesia), a new battery pack being inserted in a pouch under the skin. The situation has improved dramatically. Though nuclear-powered batteries have proved disappointing, lithium-powered batteries now may last from seven to ten years. Battery life is monitored by the so-called magnet rate (elicited by holding a magnet over the battery pouch); this rate decreases slightly, but perceptibly, as battery life declines until a predetermined target rate is reached, which signals the need for replacement. Transtelephonic monitoring of pacemakers, routine and convenient, helps forecast battery failure. Miniaturization has been applied to pacemakers, too: current battery units for adults may be as thin as one-quarter inch and two inches or smaller in diameter; their weight has shrunk from several ounces to less than one ounce. And units can be small enough for the occasional infant who is born in need of a pacemaker.

Though pacing wires from the battery of the pacemaker can be sewn into the heart muscle itself, this requires opening the chest. Now, most frequently, pacing wires are threaded along a vein into the right ventricle until the tip of the wire engages the muscle network lining that chamber. The battery itself is implanted in a skin pouch nearby and the wires course through a small tunnel under the skin from the battery to the vein.

Pacemaker circuitry has become more flexible, hence more complex. Early pacemakers fired *only* at a steady "fixed" rate; newer models "sense" any temporary return (even a single beat) of the patient's own heart rhythm and cut out when not needed; this saves battery life and avoids competition between the pacemaker and the heart's inherent rhythm. Moreover, sophisticated models, in cases of A-V node disease, now can "track" the patient's own inherent sinus node impulses and electronically bypass the A-V node, ensuring both a normal heart rate and contraction pattern—normally, the atria contract just before the ventricles—a feature that can be especially helpful in active young people.

Most pacemaker units now inserted are "programmable" by the doctor. Several features, notably the pacing rate, can be varied for optimal performance, utilizing a radio-frequency programmer that, in effect, speaks to the pacemaker through the intact skin. The doctor can "interrogate," or monitor, the pacemaker to learn whether its battery needs changing.

Overall, the most common reason for insertion of a pacemaker today is in cases of *default* of the sinus node, known as the sick-sinus syndrome. These patients, most often elderly, usually come to the physician for one of two reasons: a very slow heart rate, which results in fainting or near-fainting—or a slow heart rate alternating with a very fast one (180 to 240 beats a minute or even faster), which can cause the same symptoms. In the latter case, as the sinus node fails, renegade pacemakers in the atria, now unregulated and sensing their chance for glory, take over and drive the heart at two or three times the normal rates. Insertion of a pacemaker can help control both extremes of heart rate; the pacemaker also allows use of drugs that might be ineffective or even hazardous without the backup that a pacemaker affords.

Pacemakers can be useful in many clinical situations. A pacemaker may be required in heart attacks (in which the sinus or A-V node may be damaged); or after trauma to the heart—a knife or bullet wound. Sometimes such damage comes, unintentionally, from the scalpel of the surgeon, as in Janet's case.

Janet is a twenty-four-year-old nurse who had an operation for a congenital hole in the heart fifteen years ago. The defect in her heart was closed successfully, but a known potential complication of such surgery occurred: Her A-V node was damaged by the operation; installation of a pacemaker proved necessary to treat the resultant slow heart rate.

Several pacemaker batteries later, Janet is doing well. But recent technology may benefit her at her next battery change. Here's why. Currently, her battery discharges at a rate of 74 regardless of her activity. This rate is perfectly fine for sleep or sitting quietly, but it's a bit too low for exertion, during which the heart rate normally speeds up to 100 or more. Pacemaker technology now suggests several answers to her problem. One of the most attractive is a battery unit that automatically *senses* the patient's *activity*—a sensor (a piezoelectric crystal, to be specific) responds to mechanical events of the body (the feet hitting the ground, for example). As a result, the pacemaker is programmed to *speed up* as more and more of these events are sensed. The faster Janet's feet move, the faster her heart is paced. Both normal-activity rates and maximum rates can be programmed or preset. Activity-sensing pacemakers were described only in 1983 but have now been implanted in more than eighty thousand patients worldwide. One of these new battery units may be just the right conductor for Janet's cardiac orchestra.

One of the most harrowing evenings of my life involved a pacemaker. I was a cardiology fellow, on call at the hospital one evening with a colleague, Loren. Loren and I were called to see an elderly man who'd just been admitted because of recurrent "spells." Just as we hooked the patient up to the EKG machine, the man's body stiffened all over; then his arms and legs began the uncontrollable flail-like movements of a full-blown seizure. His EKG provided the explanation. His heart rate had fallen precipitously from a normal 80 beats a minute down to 20 beats a minute. His sinus node kept on conducting, but his A-V node wasn't paying the least bit of attention: his ventricles reverted to their own slow inherent rate of 20, an inadequate rate for perfusion of his brain, which led to the seizures. As we watched, giving the man oxygen and trying to prevent him from injuring himself during the seizure, his normal heart rate suddenly returned and his seizure stopped. Several more spells followed in rapid succession. They came on as unpredictably as lightning and, as they came, the patient entered, again and again, the dark cave of unconsciousness. Then, just as unpredictably as the slow heart rate had come, it abated; the man's pulse rate picked up, and he began to revive, groggy, disoriented, and combative. Clearly, the patient needed a temporary pacemaker.

All this took place before the newer technology that allows a pacemaker wire to be "floated" into place in the heart at the bedside. Loren and I were faced with the necessity of getting the patient down to the X-ray department so we could use fluoroscopy to help position the pacemaker within the heart. On the elevator down to

X-ray, the man had another spell. Loren and I were better prepared for this one. We knew that a slow heart rate may be temporarily "paced" by the rhythmic thumping of a physician's closed fist on the patient's chest (the mechanical thumps are translated into small electrical impulses). In this desperate situation, I doubled my fist and struck the man forcefully on the chest wall over the heart. This crude caveman approach worked! By thumping the man's chest repetitively, once a second (which, at the time, he didn't appreciate at all), we kept his heart rate up and staved off the life-threatening seizures. In the X-ray department, one of us thumped intermittently while the other worked feverishly to open a vein. Between thumps, we finally managed to thread a pacemaker into the vein. In the dusk of the X-ray room, our eyes glued to the monitor, we watched the pacemaker snake back toward—and into—the heart, bringing some much-needed external electricity to bear on the man's own failing electrical apparatus.

While browsing the display section at a large cardiology meeting recently, I passed a booth in which a young man was extolling the merits of his company's pacemakers. When I looked closer, I could see, under the man's opened shirt, two large conducting pads on his chest; they were connected by wires to a monitor behind him. For demonstration purposes, he was pacing his own (normal) heart *externally,* just as we'd done for Mr. Trammell twenty-seven years ago: today this can be done virtually painlessly (the large pads are part of the reason). One obvious result: Ambulance personnel can utilize such equipment quickly, on the scene, to bring a slow heart rate back up to normal on the way to the hospital. Such a lifesaving technique is just one more example of how far we've come when caring for a person whose own heart rate can't quite keep up with the music of the world.

The Frozen Room

For two months of every year, April and December, I'm assigned to the cardiology consultation service of a large county hospital. The cardiology fellows who work with me are uniformly bright, and in their fourth or fifth year of training after medical school. They don't miss much. The fellows see the patients first, then present them to me for examination and discussion on afternoon rounds. My role is to say something wise.

Rounds take us all over the hospital, from the psychiatry service to obstetrics, from surgery to dermatology, wherever hearts are sick.

The modern hospital is a complicated place, full of kingdoms, replete with many rulers; one of the most benevolent is Charles. I like to think of his work as a lifelong study of suspended animation.

$\mathcal{T}$his is the room in which the body confesses. My friend Charles, the pathologist, is resident soothsayer here. He calls it "the frozen room." Charles and I are here early, in this small room across from the surgical suites. The operating rooms, connected by a maze of cool tile, are patrolled by nurses, physicians, and technicians in blue-clad camaraderie, seriously joyful and absorbed just now in putting the world to sleep.

The frozen room is not: it is warm—the metabolism of five refrigerators is responsible for the heat. In a way, the temperature befits the place; the room is one of the hot seats within the hospital. Here, surgical specimens are examined while the surgeon waits impatiently and the patient sleeps on.

A resident and a technician have now joined Charles and me in the room, which is about fifteen feet square; a large "pass-through" refrigerator occupies much of the wall across from the operating suites. Usually, a voice over the intercom announces the arrival of a specimen; then, the refrigerator door on the opposite side slides open and the pathologist's work begins. Close by, a "teaching micro-scope" holds out arms that sprout five binocular "heads," enabling five people to examine the same tissue at once. One of the heads projects toward a small booth in which a surgeon can seat himself to consult with the pathologist. This booth has come to be known as "the confessional."

Generally, when a surgical specimen is sent to pathology, "permanent" slides are made, not "frozen sections." Permanent slides require a full day for processing and additional time for interpretation, which can take up to three days. The procedure is a more leisurely one, the stakes not as immediately high for either pathologist or patient.

In contrast, a frozen section takes only a few minutes; the technique is designed to provide immediate guidance for the surgeon. The pathologist in the frozen room works toward an either-or decision: he says yes, this tissue is malignant, or no, it's not. Either answer dictates the direction in which the operation will then proceed. But it's not always so simple.

Mr. Graham has had gradually increasing hoarseness for several weeks. His ENT (ear, nose, and throat) surgeon has already diagnosed cancer of the larynx and has just now removed tissue for frozen section. First, Charles inspects the tissue, looking for suspicious areas. He cuts a small piece and places it in a clear embedding fluid on a small metal platform about one inch square in size. The tissue is then frozen in one of several ways, most commonly by simply placing it for a minute or two on a metal surface in one of the freezing units, which turns it frost-white. Freezing can be hastened by spraying the surface with a pressurized fluorocarbon; this is not done as often now because of concern about the ozone layer. (I pick up the can and note, with some surprise, that it's produced by an automobile radiator supply company.) Once the tissue is frozen, a microtome is used to shave off translucent slivers, which are then transferred to glass slides and immediately sent through a series of "baths": a fixative; two types of stain (one dyes the nucleus of the cells a deep purple, the other confers a pink tint to the remainder of the cell, the cytoplasm); then alcohol, to remove the water; and finally, xylene, which gives off a pungent odor not unlike that of nail-polish remover. Charles says wryly, "We'll probably find out one day that smelling xylene all the time causes leukemia or something."

Charles takes the slide to the "driver's seat" of the many-headed microscope. The rest of us peer down the binocular eyepieces. Charles's eyes travel across the slide like those of a truck driver on a familiar road: precisely because it *is* familiar, he knows where to look for trouble. One of the pathologist's problems is knowing *the range of normal*; he must take into account the tissue changes caused by the freezing. And he must be skilled at recognizing certain, sometimes unexpected, infections in tissues (e.g., tuberculosis and fungal infections). If the answer is not a clear yes or no, he must make a "judgment call" based on subtleties of the microscopic landscape. The intercom interrupts us: the surgeon wants to come around to the confessional and consult with Charles.

While we are waiting for the surgeon, another case is ready. The tissue is a breast lump from a young woman. We look at the slide as Charles's eyes sweep over it. He points out extensive fibrous (scar) tissue, all stained pink, with small islands of breast tissue dotting it. As Charles says, "miles and miles of Sahara with an occasional oasis here and there." He takes a closer, high-powered look at the breast tissue itself: "See the epithelial cells lined up like soldiers?" Yes, I see. There is *organization* here, unlike the disarray of cancer. "Oh, good," Charles mutters, "I'm beginning to feel better about this." The discovery is all his; in this long moment, he is the only person in the world with the answer. He jots down a few words of diagnosis and calls the surgeon to tell him the tissue is not malignant. As he hangs up, he points out the merciful side of the frozen room: "The patient will know, as soon as she wakes up," Charles says, "that she doesn't have cancer—she won't have to wait for the permanent slides to find out."

The surgeon now seats himself in the confessional. Charles has identified the expected signs of cancer of the larynx. But the surgeon is most interested in the "margin" of the tissue: has he removed all the cancer? Charles moves the slide steadily toward the surgical edge of the tissue.

Despite the fact that the tissue around the tumor looked normal to the naked eye, cancer cells march right up to the margin. The surgeon, his forehead sweating under his blue cap, sits for a full minute before he speaks: "We'll just have to take out some more, that's all." Thirty minutes later, the medical student on the case brings around additional tissue for study. This time, the margin is free of tumor. The surgeon can now finish the case, don his white coat, and talk with the patient's family, telling them truthfully, "We believe we got it all."

A major advance in surgery for skin cancer is a technique called Mohs' surgery (named for the surgeon who developed it). It uses frozen sections to identify tumor-free margins: this enables the physician to remove enough tissue so that the cure rate approaches 100 percent, but no more than necessary, so that disfigurement of the patient is minimized.

Our next case is from a man with prostatic cancer. The CAT scan, with its unerring vision, has identified a mass next to the enlarged prostate. The mass, just now removed, turns out, under the microscope, to be a lymph node that has been invaded by the cancer. Small dark bodies, nucleoli, lodged within the nuclei of the cells, resemble prominent "eyes." As Charles points out, "Prostate cancer always looks back at you like that."

The cases are coming fast now. The slides are from a vast array of tissues: ovary, parathyroid, salivary gland, peritoneum, bowel. My travels with Charles are beginning to blur in my mind. I think of nothing medical now: I think of art. Of the dripped and splattered canvases of Jackson Pollock, arrayed in disarray, as random and energetic as cancer. And the furled and fluted flowers of Georgia O'Keeffe, seen closer than anyone ever thought to see them before.

Last year, at the age of forty-four, Charles finally got to the National Gallery in Washington. It was Rembrandt who impressed him most: "I realized then what real art is." When he entered medical school, he never dreamed he'd end up in pathology, nor did his mother. "I always thought the pathologists were a little strange," he says; "I thought I'd go back to my hometown and practice family medicine." He took a medical-pediatric internship, but remembered, with pleasure, pathology in medical school and gave it a try; then came several years of pathology residency. He's been busy since in a career especially distinguished for teaching. As for his mother, he thinks she has a pretty good idea now as to what he does all day and, he says, she is "convinced that I do play a role in medical care!" She's pleased that he doesn't do as many autopsies now as he used to do: the need for them has diminished as more accurate premortem diagnosis (by CAT scan–guided biopsy, for example) is possible. (Still, autopsies provide critical information in some cases and can aid in the discovery of new or previously undescribed diseases.) The nature of Charles's work has changed in other ways over the years: when he was younger, the work was more impersonal. Now, increasingly, the tissues he examines are from people he knows, from other physicians, from personal friends. He recalls for me, with special poignance, the day an eminent surgeon showed up unannounced at the frozen room during his wife's surgery for cancer. The diagnosis was clear to both as they pored over the slide. Afterward, the surgeon thanked Charles and retreated to the waiting room, once more simply one of the family waiting for the report.

Has he made mistakes in the frozen room? "Oh, sure," Charles says, "you can't help making some. I try to err on the side of benignity; the worst mistake is to misread something that's benign and call it malignant: you can't undo surgery that's already been done. But sometimes the permanent slides will make the diagnosis of cancer when the frozens were not clear. We don't like to do this, but one can always go back and do more extensive surgery if the permanent sections dictate it."

The frozen room seems warmer than when we started.

The technician has been wearing a button on her coat all morning, but I haven't been able to read it until just now: *Enjoy life. This is not a dress rehearsal.* In her three years in the frozen room, she has learned her lesson well.

One of the standard texts of surgical pathology recommends that the pathologist follow up his cases when the diagnosis on the slide is not clear: the book states, "Time is often a better diagnostician." True enough. But the frozen room is still the place to be when time is precisely what one doesn't have.

PART THREE
The Common Room

◈

Balloon Man

◈

The word *balloon* has at least two antecedents from the French, both of them related to the dance:

> *ballonne*:   a wide circular jump in ballet
>
> and *ballon*:   the lightness of movement that exaggerates the duration of a ballet dancer's leap

Who would have thought such an etymology would lead to the heart?

$\mathcal{I}$n his poem that begins "in Just-spring," e. e. cummings speaks of the beguiling "balloonman [who] whistles far and wee." In 1980, when I first met Andreas Gruentzig, a real-life balloon man, I thought of that line. Dr. Gruentzig was a pioneer, the first person to work therapeutically *within* the coronary arteries, a feat of considerable derring-do. This year, in the United States, more than 200,000 balloon dilatations of the coronary arteries will be done, using the technique developed by Gruentzig (who emigrated from Zurich to Atlanta in 1980). Physically, Andreas had a certain resemblance to Errol Flynn, the cinematic risk-taker: he was slender, with penetrating eyes, a ready smile, and a mustache that made him seem both *gal*lant and gal*lant*. As cummings would have said, "Jesus, he was a handsome man. . . ." Physical features and charisma aside, though, Andreas Gruentzig was a world-class scientist, who gave full credit to those who had preceded him: Werner Forssmann, for example.

In 1929, Forssmann, a twenty-five-year old German physician, was assigned to a small clinic in Eberswalde. He was convinced that the heart could be entered safely with a small tube or catheter. His superior had forbidden such dangerous research, but the impatient young man began anyway. In order to obtain sterile instruments, he needed the help of a nurse. As part of a ruse, he persuaded a nurse to let him try the procedure on *her*. After she'd obtained the sterile tray he needed and had stretched out on the operating

table, Forssmann strapped her down so she couldn't inter-
fere. He then sterilized his *own* arm, and using local
anesthesia, made an incision near the elbow and isolated one
of his veins; the tube slid in easily, to its total length of
twenty-six inches, far enough to reach the interior of his
heart. He felt no pain, he said, only a feeling of "warmth"
behind his collarbone as the catheter slid along under it.
Forssmann then released the incredulous nurse and the two
walked down several flights to an X-ray room. The tube
was, indeed, in the heart. Research based on this courageous
self-experiment began, but twenty-seven years passed before its full impact was recognized. In 1956, along with Drs.
André Cournand and Dickinson Richards (who applied
Forssmann's work to patients), Forssmann was awarded the
Nobel prize. Of this honor, he is reported to have said, "I
feel like the village parson who has just learned that he has
been made bishop."

In the early 1960s, Drs. C. T. Dotter and M. P. Judkins
of the University of Oregon devised a technique to open
narrowed vessels in the leg by passing progressively larger
dilating catheters past the obstruction. Meanwhile, Dr.
Mason Sones, at the Cleveland Clinic, had shown that the
coronary arteries could be safely and selectively injected
with dye, leading to much-improved diagnosis. The medical woods are full of risk-takers, something disease often
requires.

This afternoon, Dr. Spencer King, director of the
Andreas Gruentzig Center at Emory, is to perform a
balloon angioplasty on a woman in her late fifties. As
Spencer and I arrive at the cath lab, the patient is already on
the table. A cardiology fellow has completed the prelimi-
naries: first, he used a needle to puncture the femoral artery
at the top of the leg. Then he passed a flexible guide wire
through the needle (which was then withdrawn); finally,
over the guide wire, an ordinary thin catheter was slipped
into the vessel. The catheter can be seen now, on fluoros-

copy, as it moves against the current in the aorta. The catheter, about three feet long, curves gently around the arch of the aorta and turns downward toward the heart and the coronary arteries. The two coronary arteries, the right and the left, have a critical function—they nourish the heart itself, taking off from the aorta just after it leaves the heart. Angiographers know where the coronary artery openings are simply by having been there so many times. In seconds, the tip of the catheter shallowly engages the opening of the right coronary artery. A brief puff of dye into the artery confirms the catheter position; the artery is "invisible" except when this dye is injected.

The patient's chest pain is caused by a narrowing in the right coronary artery. The narrowed segment is rather long, nearly an inch, which can lead to technical problems—the mortal clay of a narrowed coronary can crack under pressure from the balloon, so the artery is approached warily. An angioplasty catheter, with an inch-long deflated balloon attached near the tip, is unpacked from its sterile wrap. This catheter, small in diameter (the size of a pencil lead) and flexible, is actually a double-barreled tube: one barrel for injection of dye and for measuring blood pressures; the other to carry a solution to inflate the balloon.

The balloon catheter is now guided into the culprit coronary artery; it is threaded gingerly past the narrowed area. The patient is asked, over and over, "Any chest pain?" because the balloon catheter itself further reduces blood flow in the artery. The balloon is now centered properly across the obstruction; blood pressures above and below the narrowing show a sixty-six-millimeter difference (the pressure being higher above the obstruction), which helps gauge the severity of the lesion and the efficacy of the treatment.

The balloon is now inflated for only a few seconds, puffing up to the shape of a sausage about an inch long and an eighth of an inch in diameter. It's then blown up again for a full minute.

When the balloon is inflated the first time, the woman has brief chest pain, but the pain passes. After the second inflation, the pressures are almost equal, as they should be, indicating that the narrowed passage has been successfully widened. Injection of dye confirms this happy fact. The angiographer's work is done, except for showing the patient, on a television replay, the before and after of her artery.

Dr. King speaks to her softly, telling her she's to remain in bed overnight on heparin, a blood thinner, to prevent clotting: if things go well, she can go home late tomorrow. Finally, she gets a last reminder from Dr. King: "Remember our agreement, now: No smoking. Ever again. Okay?"

"Okay," she replies, grinning a relieved smile at me.

It was Andreas Gruentzig's genius to recognize the potential of the balloon catheter. In the early 1970s, at the University Hospital of Zurich, he worked tirelessly to develop catheters and balloons using different materials to enhance flexibility and thinness. He then used these balloon catheters to open vessels that are larger in diameter than the coronary arteries, such as those to the kidneys and the legs. Finally, in September 1977, he identified an appropriate patient, a man with angina due to a single narrowed artery. After seven years of work, Andreas Gruentzig was ready to take on the coronary arteries.

A contingency plan was in effect: If something went wrong, a surgical team was ready to perform an emergency bypass of the vessel. In fact, that day there were several prominent onlookers in the cath lab, including the chiefs of surgery and cardiology. To Dr. Gruentzig's relief, though the narrowing in the artery was severe, the catheter slipped by it relatively easily. The balloon was inflated twice for short periods, following which the pressure below the narrowed area had increased nicely. Injection of dye showed that the artery had opened. History had been made.

A few months later, after performing the operation on four additional patients, Gruentzig shared his triumph with the medical world in a paper to the British medical publication *Lancet*. Thereafter, people from all over the world came, first to Zurich, and, beginning in 1980, to Atlanta, to discuss the problems and potential of this new technique. Over the next few years, Gruentzig and his colleagues performed several thousand angioplasties. The technique was demonstrated and taught to hundreds of cardiologists in postgraduate courses. (The courses utilize a huge video screen and voice-over communications between the "operator" in the cath lab and the audience of several hundred in the auditorium.)

Much research continues today—for example, lasers are being tested as a supplement to the balloon technique. Answers to many questions are being sought, among them whether angioplasty or bypass surgery is better in a given patient. Angioplasty is quicker and less traumatic than bypass surgery (which requires opening of the chest). But arterial narrowing recurs in perhaps 25 percent of patients after angioplasty, a problem that has not yet been solved (angioplasty *can* be repeated in such patients). And premier angioplasty labs need to have a surgical team on standby for emergencies that might occur, an expensive proposition.

Unfortunately, Andreas Gruentzig was not destined to hear the answers to these questions. The world has a special place in its collective memory for those who die young, a group to which Dr. Gruentzig and his physician–wife were added on October 27, 1985; they were killed when the plane he was piloting crashed on a flight from the coast of Georgia to Atlanta. He was forty-six years old.

Not long ago, I received a letter from one of Dr. Gruentzig's grateful patients. I include an excerpt from it, all the more interesting because of what it tells us, from the patient's point of view, about this medical pioneer. She'd had an angioplasty; hers was "a difficult case." The procedure went well. However, several hours after it, she began to have bleeding into her right leg (from the arterial puncture). Her letter continues, ". . . my blood pressure dropped; and something had to be administered to stop the bleeding in spite of the risk of a clot. Unfortunately, I threw a clot and had to be rushed back in for a repeat angioplasty, which succeeded. That was all special enough. Andreas Gruentzig had saved my life.

"But to add to the specialness, he stood in the intensive care unit, in a beautiful leather coat, dressed for an evening out, and applied hand pressure to the right leg, which had caused the difficulty. My sense of time is poor. You will know better than I how long he must have stood there. . . . My husband and son stood by, feeling helpless, but knowing what wonderful hands I was in. We talked about his work and mine and the experience I had just had. He was as charming and thoughtful as he was talented. When he left for his party, he kissed my hand."

In September 1987, ten years to the day after that first historic angioplasty in Zurich, the original patient came to Emory for doctors to have another look at his arteries. There was considerable drama in the moment, made more poignant because of Dr. Gruentzig's death. In the words of Spencer King's secretary, "Dr. King injected the dye . . . and on the big screen came this wonderful picture of arteries that looked—I hope mine look as good as his were—and the whole audience was just so stunned by this finding and everyone burst into applause." It was a haunted moment, one that Andreas Gruentzig would have cherished and perhaps followed with a brief bow.

Danger in the Dining Room

[the robin] sang
i have a good digestion
and there is a god after all
which i was wicked
enough to doubt
yesterday when it rained
breakfast breakfast
i am full of breakfast
and they are at breakfast
in heaven
they breakfast in heaven
all s well with the world
so intent was this pious and
murderous robin
on his own sweet song
that he did not notice
mehitabel the cat
sneaking toward him . . .

from "the robin and the worm"
by Don Marquis

$\mathcal{I}$ ride in the squad car to the apartment complex where he lived. I can now reconstruct the scene: He is old and lives alone. It is noon, Sunday. I imagine that he slept late because, ostensibly, at least, there is not that much to get up for. His dentures are broken—or he's simply not bothered to put them in yet. He's hungry. He goes to the icebox, takes out an already opened can of peach halves. He spoons up a peach half, smooth, still bathed in its slick sweet syrup; he pops it into his mouth, wondering what else he can rustle up for breakfast. Meanwhile, the peach: there are no dentures to help control the movement of the slippery bolus within his mouth, to keep it from moving backward toward the larynx. With no warning and with terrible finality, the man is suddenly choking. Nor can he utter a cry for help. The neighbors hear nothing; they find him, unconscious and brain-dead, perhaps thirty minutes later. He's brought by ambulance to the emergency department, where the correct diagnosis is made. As the laryngoscope is used to lift the tongue out of the way, there is the spongy yellow mass of the peach, completely blocking the airway. Innocuous to the eye the mythic fruit—but deadly in the mouth.

Of the ways by which we can exit this mortal coil, none has, for most of us, the same savage terror as suffocation. Anyone—that is, most everyone—who has strangled momentarily when a sip of liquid "went down the wrong way" has experienced some measure of that terror. I have wit-

157

nessed the deaths of patients by slow suffocation when cancer invaded their bronchial trees. Such deaths must resemble a long dream during which you wake from time to time to find the assailant still holding the pillow forcibly over your face. The heart can be much more merciful: When it makes a peremptory decision to cease and desist, the brain receives the telegram instantly and lays down its arms without a struggle.

As children, we tried to see how long we could hold our breath: even the champion finally had to give up. It's not possible, therefore, for us to conceive of taking in a breath that we can't let go of, even as we stretch vainly, dizzily toward the next sharp inrush of air. Breathing is the kind of thing only children experiment with: by the time we're adults, we've put breathing out of our minds. Perhaps it's because we are able to breathe so forgetfully, because the respiratory center is always so dependably on automatic, that to drown oneself is no easy matter. As long as one can swim and has the energy to, there is a supreme reluctance to take that first and last deep breath of water: Virginia Woolf with stones in her pocket was the exception. The thought is one worthy of Poe. My chest tightens as I write this. Hunger for air is deep and deeply mortal—or so I had always thought.

The most extraordinary café coronary I've ever seen was not in the dining room or the kitchen, not in the emergency department, but at a lake south of Atlanta. I was on my way down to the boathouse when I met a man coming up from the dock, carrying an obviously heavy, bulging plastic bag. I asked what kind of fishing day he'd had, and in answer to the question, he opened the bag. A most remarkable sight emerged. A widemouth bass peered up at me, its walleyes still looking a bit terrified (as do all fish eyes to city boys). But its awesome, wide mouth was incredibly full of duck—to be precise, the lower half of a duck, quite drowned. Clearly, the fish had suffered an aquatic café coronary. The bass, submarining silently below, had spotted the duck and greedily envisioned a week's worth of food all at once. It had then attempted what can only be considered a truly heroic bite. Lunging upward, the bass had attempted to engulf, then ingest, the duck. Above, below, and all around them was mutual doom: breath and death on one tether. Their struggle must have been ferocious, but to no avail, like fingers trapped in a Chinese puzzle. All the fisherman had to do was to scoop from the water the floating hapless pair of Sunday dinners. I do not mean to make light of what is a very serious subject. But I, like doubting Thomas, have seen, felt, and believed.

A poet friend, several years ago, knowing of my interest in such subjects, wrote me the following harrowing tale: "We came very close to a real tragedy a week ago. Elaine [not her real name] and I went to a party, very large, maybe a hundred people. In the course of the evening, I saw her groping toward the bathroom, making horrible choking noises. I thought she was just sick and asked if I should get a doctor as I showed her to a bathroom. She just sort of made a sign that I should. When I walked through three rooms, found a doctor, and got back to the bathroom, she was lying in the tub in that proverbial pool of blood. Hardly breathing. What happened was she had choked on a piece of meat, and at first tried to be polite and not show it, and then lost consciousness in the bathroom, fell, and cut her scalp. Thank God there was a doctor at the party—two, in fact. He dislodged the piece of meat, called us an ambulance, and she had sixteen stitches. She was pretty scared, naturally. The doctor said she could have died without help. And since, we've heard at least five stories about this one or that one who choked and died right at the dinner table. *Chew your food!*"

The above letter was written a number of years ago, at a time when the café coronary was just beginning to be recognized for the special characteristics of its lethality: a party; alcohol (which depresses the cough reflex); a tough piece of steak; sometimes ill-fitting dentures. The victim of a café coronary may rise from the table clutching his chest or lower throat; but, most importantly, the feature that differentiates his choking from a true heart attack is that he cannot *speak*.

Out of embarrassment, people with airway obstruction almost always try to leave the room—someone should always stay with them. Lives of choking victims are saved daily now through the application of simple techniques such as the Heimlich maneuver. Raising the pressure in the abdomen and chest can pop the obstruction out of the airway much like the cork from a champagne bottle. The bystander must learn to use such maneuvers reflexly and within minutes. They must be etched on our brains and ready at a moment's notice: it is not enough to mount the rules on the walls of restaurants.

> *"But wait a bit," the Oysters cried,*
> *"Before we have our chat;*
> *For some of us are out of breath*
> *And all of us are fat!"*
>> *"The Walrus and the Carpenter"*
>> *—Lewis Carroll*

Choking is not the only danger of the dinner table. There is also obesity, always lurking ominously, and, in the glint of the silverware, the gleam of the plates, there may even be the ghost of gluttony. As one who has confronted squarely (or roundly) a certain tendency to corpulence myself, I can never forget the astonishing case of Michael, on which I look back today with even greater pathos than when I first and last saw him, years ago.

Michael was big to begin with. He was born big, to large parents; for whatever reason, he began eating as an infant and stopped only for death. Again, the call came over the radio—this time from the fire department. Michael had been treated at the hospital some years before, for a minor ailment; he weighed three hundred pounds then. But now Michael was ill, very short of breath, and he needed to be brought in to the hospital by the fire department. But there were logistical problems. Over the last few years of his life, Michael's appetite regulation had gone completely out of control. He had literally eaten himself into his own room, from which he never ventured because of his own inability to maneuver. Doting relatives brought in food and he grew more and more obese.

The firemen were not prepared for what they found. No one could have been. Over the years, Michael had become one with his room; there was little space left for anyone else, much less several firemen. No matter where they walked in the room, Michael was always closer to them than any ordinary person would have been. He dominated the room like Michelangelo's David, but tragically overgrown; as he sat, propped up on an oversized couch, he filled the canvas around him better than Gertrude Stein did for Picasso. He loomed: metabolism personified, alpha and omega, many words made flesh, a continent, an enormous grab of gravity clad in a tentlike blue bathrobe that seemed to be reflected in his blue lips. He was breathing heavily—one breath had no sooner left off than another was impatient to begin.

An ordinary stretcher would not bear Michael's weight, nor would he fit on one. The firemen were unable to get through the door to the room with a larger bed. Finally, after some discussion, the door frame itself was removed to enlarge the entrance. The door was taken down and Michael was stretched out on that, placed with some difficulty in the back of a flatbed truck, and brought to the emergency department. I talked to him briefly. He was distinctly uncomfortable, short of breath, speaking in short, gasping sentences. I asked him what had been bothering him. He replied, ironically, that during the past week or so, he'd lost his appetite. I mourned for him as he said that sentence. His weight was estimated at seven hundred and fifty pounds, but there was no way to take an actual reading: Michael could not stand for one, nor were scales available to read that high. I remember noticing that a silver ring on the small finger of his left hand was overgrown with pudgy folds, like a piece of wire circling and embedded in a sapling.

We were in the process of moving Michael to two hospital beds lashed together when he suddenly gasped, became much bluer, and died. The exact cause of his death, in his mid-thirties, could have been one of many. But I am obliged to think of the true underlying cause by the Latin name, so true in Michael's case: *adiposa dolorosa*.

All this was almost twenty years ago. Michael, had he lived, would find himself these days the modern counterpart of the Elephant Man, perhaps even more alienated, even more closely confined to his room. The present time is a particularly difficult one in which to be so excessively overweight. Ours is the age of slimness, fad diets, of aerobics, jogging, and of an almost obsessional commitment to physical health.

Ironically, new approaches to our understanding of anorexia and its sister malady, bulimia, are helping us penetrate the mysteries of appetite, its regulation, and dysfunctions, even as we explore the roles of exercise, digestion, and metabolism in such patients. Meanwhile, we in medicine should admit that there is much we do not know about cases like Michael's. There's an old saying, "The opera isn't over until the fat lady sings." Until we better understand precisely what goes on in the dining room, some operas will end prematurely because there is, sadly, no breath left for the song.

Why Some Hands
Get So Cold

In Act One of Puccini's opera *La Bohème*, Rodolfo, a poet, is ostensibly helping Mimi, a beautiful but sick woman, search for the key to her apartment. Rodolfo, in fact, quickly finds the key, but conceals this discovery from Mimi. In the process of continuing this "search," Rodolfo touches Mimi's hand, following which he sings one of the most famous of all arias, "Che gelida manina" ("Your tiny hand is frozen"). Had Rodolfo had medical training, he most certainly would have considered the possibility that Mimi had a common circulatory disturbance, as we shall see.

$\mathcal{U}$ntil last fall, Carolyn had no idea anything was wrong. She considered it a nuisance that, in a cool room, her hands might tingle and feel numb for a few minutes, or turn pale or blue. Lots of people have cold hands. But her friend's comment at a football game alarmed her: "Your hands are so white! They look like they don't have any blood in them!" Carolyn phoned her physician, who listened to her story. "What could this be?" she asked. "It could be Raynaud's syndrome," he said, and went on to explain.

Raynaud's, a common problem that basically is an exaggerated sensitivity to cold, can be a devilish malady—no more unjust than other chronic illnesses, perhaps; and, by itself, not life-threatening. But it has, for me, a mythic quality, like a penance imposed by a vengeful god, with its relentless interdictions on body and spirit, its daily prohibitions. It makes it impossible for many of its sufferers to enjoy activities the rest of us take for granted—throwing a snowball in the winter, swimming in the summer.

Maurice Raynaud, a French physician, described Carolyn's symptoms in 1862. Raynaud's (pronounced *ray-noze*) is a widespread problem: one study estimates its prevalence at between 1.9 percent and 4.6 percent of the population, depending on criteria used. It involves the small blood vessels of the fingers, especially, and occurs in episodes that are triggered by exposure to cold (an air-conditioned room can do it) or emotional stress. In a typical Raynaud's attack,

165

which lasts from a few to several minutes, patients complain of coldness, numbness or tingling, and *color changes* in the fingers (less commonly in the toes, and occasionally in the ears or nose). These are parts of the body, at the outer reaches of the circulatory system, most likely to be exposed to cold, the ones most subject to frostbite in everyone. Color changes in Raynaud's can be dramatic, from extreme whiteness (pallor) to blueness (cyanosis) and finally to redness (rubor). These "classic" changes are not always present, but when they occur they do indicate what's going on. The whiteness is caused by spasm in the vessels supplying the area, which reduces blood flow. The blueness that follows results from sluggish blood flow through vessels now filled with darker, poorly oxygenated blood. Then redness occurs during the overwarming of the area at the end of the attack, as the body overcompensates with exuberant blood flow.

We now know much more about Raynaud's than Maurice Raynaud did. Although the basic cause of the ailment is not understood in all patients, we have learned how to help treat and prevent attacks. We know, too, about the company, or lack of company, Raynaud's may keep. Clinically, it comes in two forms. One form, called primary Raynaud's (or Raynaud's disease), occurs as an isolated condition—no underlying or associated medical problems can be identified in these patients. The other form, secondary Raynaud's, may be the more serious one; it is so named because a number of conditions occur with it, or cause it.

The distinction between primary and secondary forms is important. For example, the secondary form can be triggered by certain drugs—stopping the drug can stop the Raynaud's. Moreover, a lengthy list of occupations may trigger secondary Raynaud's, important from both personal and occupational-safety points of view. With these two types of Raynaud's in mind, let's find out more about Carolyn.

Carolyn's physician took a detailed history; he performed a careful physical exam, paying special attention to the skin, hands, and feet, and the pulses. These findings were combined with the results of several blood tests. The doctor was able to tell Carolyn that, in all likelihood, she had *primary* Raynaud's—no evidence of other medical problems was found. The great majority (perhaps 90 percent) of patients fall into this more benign category. Most are women and most, like Carolyn, can't date the onset of symptoms precisely. Mild symptoms may have been overlooked for years and recognized only in retrospect. In primary Raynaud's, episodes usually begin before the age of forty, frequently before thirty years. The problem is not generally considered to be inherited, though familial cases are not infrequent. Usually the disease is symmetrical and bilateral, involving the same fingers, for example, in *both* hands. In up to 40 percent, the toes may be affected as well.

The outlook for primary Raynaud's is good. Symptoms improve over time in fully a third of patients; in some the symptoms disappear entirely. Commonsense practices for avoidance of cold are helpful, whether the Raynaud's is primary or secondary. One obvious recommendation is for Carolyn to dress warmly, using layers of clothing for insulation. Keeping the chest warm is important—the body reacts to "central" warmth by shifting blood to cooler peripheral areas and the fingers benefit. Lined gloves are good, mittens even better because the fingers warm one another. Earmuffs and muffler complete the prescription. Battery-powered warming socks and chemical "heaters" (small soft heating pouches that are worn in gloves, boots, or shoes and stay warm for hours) can provide warmth for cold-weather events.

Indoors, simple adaptations to the daily routine can work. One physician I know suggests that his patients sew magnets into cotton gloves to keep them handy on the refrigerator when they must handle ice or cold containers. Patients often find their own solutions—the use of insulated drinking glasses; sleeping in mittens; always carrying along a sweater, just in case. One source suggests that a good breakfast can help prevent Raynaud's attacks in some people: the suggestion makes sense—a low blood sugar triggers adrenaline release, which, in turn, causes constriction of small vessels. Nicotine also reduces blood flow to the digits and thus should be strictly avoided.

Biofeedback techniques have been found to be helpful in some patients with Raynaud's. Put simplistically, using biofeedback helps you to increase the temperature of your fingers by thinking warm thoughts. Some relaxation techniques may also help, which is not surprising since emotions and reactions to stress may play an important role in triggering Raynaud's attacks.

Carolyn's physician had to qualify his good news in only one respect. Though her tests showed no evidence of conditions linked to secondary Raynaud's, some of these conditions may be slow (up to several years) in making their appearance. In a small number of cases, only the passage of time can differentiate between primary and secondary forms. Hence, all patients with Raynaud's should be seen periodically by their physicians. Nevertheless, it was proper for her physician to reassure Carolyn; reassurance is an important part of the therapy.

The clinical picture in *secondary* Raynaud's differs in important ways from that seen with the primary form. Raynaud's in a male is *most often* of the secondary variety, for example, although women sufferers still outnumber males. Secondary Raynaud's may start later—after the age of fifty—than the primary form. It may also start more abruptly, occur on one side only (or one finger only), and be more severe.

As a result of impaired blood flow, ulcerations or small painful sores at the tips of the fingers or toes are considerably more common (and more often troublesome) in the secondary variety. Patients who have a tendency to develop such sores should be especially careful to avoid even minor injury to the fingers. Any infection should be treated promptly. Some people with more severe Raynaud's consider moving to a warmer climate; this can help in some cases. But emotional stress and air-conditioning, both of which may trigger blood-vessel spasms, tend to be ubiquitous and may still induce attacks.

Secondary Raynaud's is associated with a lengthy list of conditions. Its most prominent category is made up of what are called "collagen vascular diseases": scleroderma, rheumatoid arthritis, and lupus. These diseases have "vasculitis" in common, a process that thickens the walls of the blood vessels, reducing blood flow. Raynaud's in such patients is due to this vessel disease *plus* vessel spasm—a combination that helps explain why, in some cases, the secondary form is more severe than the primary.

Sometimes, secondary Raynaud's can be linked to the person's occupation, a phenomenon known as "white finger" or "vibration white finger." Workers at risk are those who habitually use tools that vibrate or otherwise sustain repetitive injury to the hands: pneumatic drills, chain saws, riveting equipment, and mining, quarrying, and grinding machines are among those implicated. The problem has also been reported in typists and pianists. Increasing debilitation has been related directly to the number of years over which the injury has occurred. Workers may lose sensation in the fingers, which become stiff or clumsy; in severe cases, gangrene, with death of the fingertips, can result.

Some drugs (nicotine has already been mentioned) can trigger secondary Raynaud's. Especially involved are those that bring about vessel constriction. One prime example is ergotamine, a drug that relieves migraine precisely by causing vessel constriction. Some of the drugs known as beta blockers, valuable in the treatment of angina or hypertension and in use by millions of patients, also cause constriction of small arteries and secondary Raynaud's.

Many other causes of secondary Raynaud's might be mentioned. The problem may herald a generalized arteriosclerotic narrowing of larger vessels. Low levels of thyroid hormone seem to cause some cases. In certain blood disorders, Raynaud's seems to result from increased "viscosity" of the blood, with "sludging" of blood cells that results in decreased flow.

Therapy for Raynaud's has improved recently. Various drugs that act to open up the small blood vessels help. Some of the newly available calcium channel blockers have shown special effectiveness. Just as nitroglycerin has been used to prevent attacks of angina, some of the calcium blockers can be useful in prevention of Raynaud's attacks, a definite step forward. But therapy for Raynaud's must be individualized; it should be reassuring that many patients with mild cases of Raynaud's, like Carolyn's, may never need drug therapy at all.

A good friend of mine has had Raynaud's syndrome for twenty years—secondary, rather severe. My views on the subject come not only from patients but from having witnessed her long encounter. She has the knack of being able to say yes in spite of the Raynaud's daily no's. Like many others with this problem, she has found some of her own solutions. She once confided to me one of her secrets: Under her designer jeans, she often wears a dowdy, but highly functional, pair of long johns. Thus, she copes. I take some comfort in the fact that the syndrome is mild for many patients—and that medical progress *is* being made. But her Raynaud's is a reminder that the world remains a much colder place for some of us than for others.

Billows of the Heart

The year 1989 was the fiftieth anniversary of *Gone With The Wind*, one of the most famous movies of any time. It was also the fortieth year after the tragic death of Margaret Mitchell, author of the book on which the movie is based. I'm often reminded of that fact as I stroll up the ambulance ramp at Grady Memorial Hospital here in Atlanta: on the wall is a plaque that reads MARGARET MITCHELL MEMORIAL EMERGENCY CLINIC. There is, of course, a story here.

In 1949, while crossing Peachtree Street (ironically, she was on her way to see a movie), Margaret Mitchell was struck by a taxi. She was brought to Grady and lay in near-coma for five days while the world press awaited word of her condition. After her death, the Mitchell family asked that, in lieu of flowers, contributions be sent to Grady Memorial Hospital. Subsequently, the emergency department was named in her honor.

I've spent many gratifying hours in that emergency department over the years, seeing patients with disturbances of heart rhythm, or chest pain—or helping residents and students interpret some of the sounds that can come from the human heart.

Some fourteen years ago, I found myself in a high school gymnasium, listening to the rambunctious hearts of maybe a hundred students who were trying out for soccer and track. I was to confirm, by a brief physical exam, that they were fit to play, and I was able to certify to the coach that the great majority of their hearts were normal. But in five students, there was more than the heart's normal "lup-dup": I could hear an extra sound, a high-pitched "click," which gave these hearts a cadence that sounded like "lup-*dit*-dup," "lup-*dit*-dup."

I referred these five students to local cardiologists for further assessment, because this extra sound suggested the condition called "mitral valve prolapse." I did speak with the parents of these students, to try to reassure them. But I'm sure my findings triggered some concern that evening—and later on—in those five households. Since then, millions of people over the world have received a diagnosis of mitral valve prolapse, now clearly the most common valve abnormality of the heart. But during this time, an undue fear, something like an international cardiac neurosis, has developed about this problem, a phenomenon recently dubbed "prolapse paranoia."

The word *prolapse* means "a slipping out of place." The term *mitral valve prolapse* was introduced in the mid-sixties to refer to a specific "billowing" of the mitral valve seen when dye was injected into the heart during cardiac catheterization. We now view mitral valve prolapse not as a single diagnostic entity but as a *spectrum* of abnormalities, *many of them quite benign and harmless*. But it's taken considerable time for cardiologists to come to this conclusion, to get our diagnostic ducks in a row. And this uncertainty on the part of physicians has spawned no small amount of anxiety among heart patients.

Mitral valve prolapse (MVP) isn't a new problem: what's new is our *understanding* and *interpretation* of it. For decades, clicks such as those I heard in the students were thought to arise *outside* the heart; they were felt to be "contact sounds" made as the heart, in its ceaseless aerobics, swivels against adjacent tissues, such as the pericardial sac that envelops it. According to this theory, which held sway until the 1960s, patients with clicks had no heart disease at all. But, in 1961, John Reid (and then J. B. Barlow and others) suggested that the mitral valve—within the heart itself—might be the source of such clicks, as well as of heart murmurs sometimes found with them. The confusion and controversy began over just what these sounds meant in terms of a healthy human heart.

In the 1960s, too, widespread use of the echocardiograph was just beginning. The cardiac echo depicts the interior of the heart using ultrasound waves, which bounce off the interior structures in definable patterns. Early Model T forms of this technology have given way, over the last thirty years, to exquisitely sensitive two-dimensional color Doppler machines, which interpret sound and distance, or dimension, the way you interpret the changing pitch of a train whistle as it fades into the distance. The echocardiogram now has become the sine qua non for the diagnosis of mitral valve prolapse. But the echo machine has also contributed to some of the uncertainty. Standardized criteria for what were *normal* sounds and normal functioning of mitral valves have been difficult to agree on. Put another way, it's been difficult, at times, to distinguish *normal* from *mildly abnormal* mitral valve function. Thus, a given patient might be told by one physician that his mitral valve was normal, only to have another physician diagnose it as a possible problem.

To understand how the mitral valve produces sounds such as clicks and murmurs, we need to look first at its normal anatomy. The job of the mitral valve is straightforward—to keep blood flowing in the proper direction within the left side of the heart. Situated between the left atrium (at the top left quarter of the heart) and ventricle (at the lower left), the valve serves as a kind of trapdoor that allows a strictly one-way cascade of blood from atrium to ventricle. Normally, the valve makes certain that the blood then makes a hairpin turn. Then, with the powerful contraction of the ventricle, it is propelled like water through a fire hose out the only escape hatch, the aortic valve, into the aorta and the rest of the circulatory system.

From the side, the two glistening-white leaflets of the mitral valve bear a rough resemblance to a miter, a ceremonial hat worn by the pope. Functionally, though, the leaflets remind me more of twin parachutes: they billow at the top and are restrained from below by tough cords or "guy wires," which, in turn, attach to (papillary) muscles in the ventricle. As the ventricle contracts, the pressure forces the sails of the mitral leaflets to "billow" up toward the atrium; overlapping at their edges, the leaflets seal tightly and prevent leakage of blood back into the atrium. When the heart relaxes, the parachutes collapse, allowing rapid flow of blood down into the ventricle.

But what happens in mitral valve prolapse? The most frequent anatomical situation is one in which the cords of the parachute are a bit too long (one or both leaflets may be elongated, thickened, or floppy, as well). In such cases, when the ventricle first contracts, the valve leaflets billow up toward the atrium as they normally do. But with the extra "play" afforded by the overgenerous length of the cords (or "chordae," as they are known medically), the leaflets suddenly "prolapse," billowing even a bit more than they normally do, extending the chordae to their full length. At that point, the movement of the leaflet is suddenly checked and it "pops" like a parachute catching the wind, causing a *click* audible with the stethoscope. Occasionally, in some people, the oversize valve may not seal perfectly and blood may leak back into the left atrium, causing a heart murmur. Some patients with MVP may have both a click and a murmur; most frequently, there is only a click.

Mitral valve prolapse occurs in two forms, designated "primary" and "secondary." The type I've just described is the primary variety; other than the abnormalities of leaflets and/or chordae, no identifiable cause can be found. A genetic or hereditary component is very likely responsible. One interesting feature of primary prolapse is that many of the patients have in common a slender body build, long graceful fingers, and a somewhat shallow chest (front to back).

Secondary prolapse may be due to a variety of cardiac diseases. For example, a heart attack may weaken one of the muscles in the ventricle and discombobulate the synchronized movements of the parachute, giving rise to a click or a murmur.

The true prevalence of MVP of either type remains uncertain. In part this is due to the slowness that existed in establishing diagnostic criteria: current more stringent criteria suggest that the incidence is lower than earlier estimates.

But other factors, not yet fully researched, may pertain: For example, how prevalence varies with ethnic group has not yet been determined. Figures from different studies have varied widely.

In Framingham, Massachusetts, a study using echo techniques found mitral valve prolapse in 4 percent of the population overall, but the condition was found to be present more often in younger people (7 percent) than older (3 percent). A striking 17 percent of the young female population in the Framingham study were found to have evidence of MVP; but the incidence declined markedly thereafter to 1 percent of the female population aged eighty or older. (Some studies have shown a higher incidence of prolapse in women than in men; others have shown an approximately equal incidence.) But one point is clear: Mitral valve prolapse is a *common* condition, whatever the actual numbers.

What we still don't know is what is the "natural history" of MVP—precisely what happens over time to the broad spectrum of patients with this diagnosis. Until such data are in, physicians must act on the best medical knowledge available, incomplete though it is.

Currently, this means that patients and physicians alike must be aware that mitral valve clicks and/or murmurs need to be followed, in part to make sure that a mitral leak doesn't appear or, if already present, worsen. Studies suggest that in up to 10 percent of patients with MVP, some progression of a mitral leak may occur.

After all, the mitral valve is subjected over a lifetime to more than three billion contractions. Given this wear and tear, a certain amount of "degenerative" change might be predicted. Therefore, on occasion, with a progressive leak, surgery to replace the mitral valve may be necessary. So, like most cardiologists, I now stress to my patients that MVP is most often a *benign* process—but it does require follow-up.

Some patients, especially those with the murmur of a mitral leak, need to take antibiotics before procedures that may inadvertently introduce bacteria into the bloodstream (dental work, for example). Antibiotics are given to sterilize the blood just as these bacteria are introduced, preventing their settling on the mitral valve and causing an infection.

A cluster of symptoms may occur in association with MVP in some patients; these patients are said to have the MVP syndrome. The symptoms may include chest pain; palpitations or irregular heart action; unusual fatigue; shortness of breath; episodic light-headedness or dizziness; and a high incidence of anxiety or "panic attacks." The symptoms may be distressing in and of themselves; furthermore, every time they occur, the patient can be reminded that there is a structural abnormality of his or her heart, no matter how mild.

We don't understand precisely why all such symptoms occur, but the link is highly likely in some patients. Treatment with beta blockers (which neutralize the effects of adrenaline on the heart) may help considerably.

Recently, at a reception for editors and writers, I fell into an amiable chat with a woman in her thirties, slender, with long, gracile fingers and a thin chest. After she learned that I was a cardiologist, she told me that just the day before she'd seen her doctor. She went on to say that her physician found "a heart murmur and told me that I have—" I interrupted her and finished her sentence: "mitral valve prolapse." She was as astonished as Hamlet was when he saw his father's ghost. I then explained to her how, because of her slender features and the frequency with which MVP occurs, I was able to make my educated guess about her problem. Physicians *have* gotten much better at diagnosis of MVP—in fact, enormous progress has been made in this area. Unfortunately, accurate prognosis—precisely what is *going to happen* as a result of the condition—has been harder to come by, a discomfiting situation for physician and patient alike.

Years ago, Gertrude Stein observed that a "rose is a rose is a rose." By now, our voluminous experience with mitral valve prolapse should emphasize to us all that a disease is *not* always a dis-ease. One fundamental duty of the physician is summed up in the Latin phrase *primum non nocere* ("first, do no harm"). As is sometimes the case in medicine, in terms of completely accurate predictions about MVP, we may be forced to wait for the medical crystal ball to clear. But the prevailing wisdom is that most patients with this condition will have a benign course.

◈

A Contemplation
of the Navel

◈

We think of the body as having *one* circulation, but there are actually *several*, each with a special purpose, each with diseases that affect it, all of them interconnected. There is the pulmonary circulation to the lungs; the systemic circulation to the body; and the lymphatic circulation involving the lymph nodes scattered throughout the body. Sometimes overlooked is that circulation which comes and goes sporadically, and often unpredictably: I'm speaking now of the placental/fetal circulation, of which the navel is the chief ornament and permanent afterthought.

$\mathcal{I}$n Greek antiquity, in the temple of Apollo at Delphi, there was a rounded stone, the *omphalos,* regarded by the ancients as the center of the world. Omphalos is the same word the Greeks used for the human navel. Leave it to Homo sapiens to locate the centrality of the universe in his own abdominal wall.

The navel is, of course, the smirk left by the umbilical cord, which is, in turn, the loose end of the thread from which our bodies were spun. Rather than navel or omphalos, most clinicians use the term *umbilicus* ("um-bi-*like*-us"). After fertilization, the ovum, in a multicelled stage called a "blastocyst," burrows into the uterine lining and ensconces itself in the area that is to become the placenta. The placenta is a specialized organ formed from both fetal and maternal tissues. The fetus is attached to the placenta by the umbilical cord, a largely vascular structure through which flow oxygen and nutrients, wastes, hormones, drugs, and some infectious agents (e.g., the AIDS virus), a process spoken of as "crossing the placenta." The fetus bobs in a heated pool, the amniotic sac, swallowing and "breathing" the fluid and periodically urinating. Amniotic fluid, though, is not stagnant but percolates continuously, so that the water is changed every three hours or so in a kind of slow-rinse laundry cycle.

The umbilical cord, then, is a two-way street between the maternal and fetal circulations. At the far end of it, the tethered fetus somersaults, tosses, and rolls like a round stone in a wheelbarrow, movements that account for the occasional, usually benign, "true knot" found in the cord. These gymnastics are gradually limited by the confines of the uterine cavity; generally, the fetus spends the last two months of pregnancy in an impressive headstand. Sound dominates this cramped (and, in the imagination, claustrophobic) place: the fetus hears, over and over, the machinery-like *whoosh-shhh* of maternal blood in the uterine arteries headed pell-mell for the placenta. No wonder the human animal likes musical rhythms.

The umbilical cord gradually elongates, until, at delivery, it's about twenty inches long. The cord contains three umbilical vessels: two arteries and a vein, all surrounded by a primitive connective tissue called "Wharton's jelly." The vessels coil around each other to form a smooth glistening structure with spirals on the outside, like a hemp rope.

During intrauterine life, the umbilical arteries carry blood from fetus to placenta; the umbilical vein ferries rejuvenated blood, with maternal oxygen and nutrients, back to the fetus. Entering the fetus, this revivified blood is allowed to bypass the essentially redundant (in terms of present function) fetal liver and lungs. At birth, though, when the cord is clamped, a series of changes occurs: some of the most dramatic take place in the lungs, which uncoil, at the first breath, like flowers in time-lapse photography. Suddenly, the fetal circulation is on its own, having been weaned, in no uncertain terms, from the "heart–lung machine" of the mother. The umbilical stump is left, stubby and weeping, ready to retract and scar down over the next few weeks. But the navel, as we'll see, is not merely a soft-shelled reminder of the sea from which we came: it has definite medical usefulness—and can be the source of medical problems. As for the umbilical vessels, remnants of them can be identified in the adult: the umbilical arteries, obliterated in part, now supply blood to pelvic structures such as the bladder; the former umbilical vein becomes an inconspicuous ligament running between the underside of the navel and the liver.

If not the center of the universe, the umbilicus *is* the center of the abdominal wall, which physicians divide, for purposes of reference, into quadrants. An imaginary plane through the navel halves the abdomen horizontally. Vertically, the abdomen is split by the thin midline *linea alba* ("white line"), a tough, fibrous structure; during pregnancy, the linea alba becomes darker and is referred to as the *linea nigra* (*nye*-grah). Two vertical *rectus* ("straight") muscles parallel each other on either side of the umbilicus, and attach to the linea: these are the muscles that ache after sit-ups.

This past summer, during an uneventful game at Fenway Park, a medical student began a small piece of research in the bleachers. He took notes as the crowd came and went for hot dogs, classifying the navels he saw as to whether they were "innies" or "outies." He needn't have bothered: that study has already been done. Many years ago, one group, commendably thorough, made plaster casts of more than a hundred navels. Then, in 1916, Dr. T. S. Cullen wrote *the* book on the umbilicus, some 680 pages' worth. The book includes drawings of sixty navels, from people of all ages. There are various shapes: horizontal (the most common), vertical, round, irregular. Most are "inner-directed," that is, "depressed." At the bottom of the navel, remnants of the retracted umbilical vessels can often be felt, in the form of a small knot. But how bizarre the body parts can seem when scrutinized! After looking at dozens of navels, up close, I felt as though *I'd* been given the once-over—by a tribe of Cyclopes.

A finger poking into the umbilicus is only a short distance from the peritoneum, the glistening, silky-thin lining of the abdominal cavity. The distance is short because there is no intervening muscle here—the rectus muscles sweep to either side—only skin, fat, and connective tissue.

This "thin spot" can lead to problems: a structure such as a bowel loop may protrude through it and result in a true hernia. But the unique anatomy also makes possible the medical procedure called "laparoscopy". In it, a slender tube (with a fiber-optic light system) is inserted through the umbilicus, often under local anesthesia, in the management of many problems, especially in gynecology. Tubal ligation is often done via laparoscopy; the technique is also valuable in the care of patients with problems as diverse as endometriosis, ectopic pregnancy, and pelvic pain.

With increased pressure within the abdomen, the umbilicus "everts" or unfolds a bit. A notable example of this occurs in pregnancy: as a friend says, "The navel pops up when the baby is done." One text encourages medical students to remember the five causes of a turned-out navel using the "five *F*'s": to wit, Fetus, Fluid, Feces, Fat, and Flatus (intestinal gas).

As the reader might suspect of a subject that warrants a 680-page book, the umbilicus commands a great deal of clinical lore in medicine. Let's begin with the term named for the author of that umbilical bible: "Cullen's sign" refers to the bluish discoloration of and around the umbilicus that may occur with intra-abdominal bleeding; he described it first in relationship to bleeding seen with ectopic pregnancy. Cullen's sign has also been called an "umbilical black eye."

The umbilicus is the "great divide" or "watershed" for the veins of the abdominal wall: veins above it drain upward, whereas those below it drain in that direction. These vessels are not usually apparent (though, during pregnancy in fair-skinned women, they may become noticeable). In cirrhosis of the liver, these abdominal veins may enlarge and distend (because their usual area for "run-off" is blocked). A cluster of dark engorged vessels may then form around the central umbilicus, a condition known as *caput Medusae* ("head of the Medusae"), named after the snake-haired monsters of Greek mythology.

During intrauterine life, there is a tubular connection, the urachus, between the umbilicus and the urinary bladder. This normally closes. If the urachus remains open, urine may be expelled through the navel into neonatal life. In a similar manner, an embryonic duct between the umbilicus and the small bowel may fail to close after birth. These distressing conditions, once detected, are correctable with surgery.

Perhaps the most famous of all signs associated with the umbilicus is the "Sister Mary Joseph nodule." Sister Mary Joseph (1856–1939) was a nurse-nun who served as first surgical assistant to Dr. W. J. Mayo of Mayo Clinic fame. (She later served with distinction as superintendent of St. Mary's Hospital in Rochester, Minnesota.) During her twenty-five years of work with Dr. Mayo, Sister Mary Joseph demonstrated superb surgical skills and judgment; she was often consulted about difficult cases. The "nodule" named in her honor is found when intra-abdominal cancer (from a variety of organs) makes its first appearance in the navel; there it may be felt as a hard lump under the skin. Unfortunately, the very presence of the nodule virtually always means that the cancer is inoperable. Nevertheless, as Dr. Mayo stresses in one report, it is a valuable sign, if for no other reason than that simple biopsy of the umbilical tissue can save the patient needless pain and expense.

In 1895, in a paper called "Umbilical Freaks," T. R. Evans referred to a young man who had virtually no navel, the skin of the area being quite flush with the abdominal wall. I leave to others the weighty question of whether Adam and Eve had navels. Though Michelangelo, stretched out under the ceiling of the Sistine Chapel, supplied an umbilicus for Adam, it seems likely that his decision was based on aesthetic, not physiologic or theologic grounds: he also provided one for God. The artist may also have felt that during his earthly travail, Adam had *earned* an umbilicus. To me, the navel winking in the center of Adam's abdomen makes him, emphatically, one of us. For the omphalos is what it always has been: center of the universe, medal of mortality, our only universal wound.

Putting the Head
and Heart to Sleep

While he was in medical school, John Keats, the Romantic poet, didn't always pay attention during class. His notes, preserved in the museum in Keats's house in London, prove it: during a lecture on the anatomy of the head, for example, Keats filled the margins of his notes with elaborate floral doodles. Medical school today is still full of lectures, some of them less than compelling. On occasion, one can find a student or two proving the truth of W. H. Auden's dictum, "A professor is someone who talks in someone else's sleep." But in Keats's day, it's safe to assume that no one slept in the surgical amphitheater, including, more often than not, the patient.

> *"The quality of mercy is not strained . . ."*
> —Shakespeare, <u>The Merchant of Venice</u>

While in London recently, I went on a pilgrimage to the operating theater of the Old St. Thomas Hospital. There are many historical reasons to visit the place; but one man's experience there constituted the main reason for my going.

John Keats (1795–1821) took his hospital training at St. Thomas. Some readers may not know that Keats studied medicine for as many years as he wrote poetry (approximately six). He was first apprenticed to the surgeon Thomas Hammond of Edmonton—an apprenticeship that lasted a full five years. During those years, Keats was very busy: it is known, for example, that he assisted in the delivery of enough babies that he was exempted from obstetrics/gynecology when he came to London for the hospital phase of his training.

The operating theater at St. Thomas was clearly part of a teaching unit: one is struck first by the "standings," the tiered aisles arranged in "horseshoe" fashion, along which students stood behind rails, maneuvering for space, trying to see the operation in progress down below. The area was inadequate for the number of students who tried to squeeze in. According to one report, there was a continual cry of "Heads, heads" as the spectators tried to see over those in front of them. John Keats, especially, would have had trouble seeing: He was just over five feet tall. What pandemonium there must have been in this place.

The operating table is wooden and narrow; during use, it was covered by a blanket, then by an oilcloth. The patient was placed on the table—the head was tilted up for comfort. Underneath the operating table was a box of sawdust that could be pushed with the foot of the surgeon to the area where blood was dripping from the oilcloth. Within the arena of the theater itself, there were chairs for distinguished visitors, a washbasin, tables, and cabinets for operating materials. Off to the side hung the surgeons' operating coats, germ-laden and ominous.

It is only a small exaggeration to say that there was *no* anesthesia during John Keats's day. The best anyone could manage was a combination of the swiftness of the surgeon, opium and alcohol in judicious amounts, and the strength of the several large men whose job was to restrain the struggling patient during his excruciating encounter.

Standing in the silent operating theater, I tried to imagine what it was like, how John Keats must have felt, watching a major surgical procedure, as the patient screamed out for mercy that was not—could not be—forthcoming.

Ultimately, Keats had to make a choice between medicine and poetry. Though in the end he chose poetry, Keats kept his medical books and continued, for the rest of his short life, to prescribe for his friends and for himself. The end was not far off. In 1820, Keats coughed up a small amount of bright red blood and said to a friend who was with him, "I know the colour of that blood; it is arterial blood: I cannot be deceived in that colour. That drop of blood is my death warrant. I must die." There followed the harrowing treatment: repeated bleedings; a semistarvation diet; and the long boat trip to Rome, where he was to die of overwhelming tuberculosis in 1821. He was twenty-five years old.

On the wall of the operating arena at St. Thomas, there

is a small chalkboard on which a visiting wag has written, in baseball-score fashion: *Surgeon 1, Patient 0.* There is much pathos in that score, of course. (There is, for me personally, some pathos as well in the score that's *implied*: Poetry 1, Medicine 0—but then, had *that* score been different, we would not have as much of Keats's poetry as we do.)

Also on the wall of the amphitheater is the Latin phrase *Miseratione non Mercede,* which means "From compassion, not for gain." No doubt the physicians of the early 1800s aimed for compassion. But how much mercy was actually possible? Effective anesthesia was decades away.

Now, back in the States, I stand in a modern operating suite, during a heart-transplant operation. The mercy of anesthesia flows freely. Let me stop the action for you with a photograph: Off in the background, the surgical team— masked, gowned, hooded, sterile, intense—hovers around the invisible patient: the whole area is draped with sterile sheets like Salome's veils. In the background, too, are the magical monitors and, hidden from view, the heart–lung machine that is pumping for and oxygenating the shrouded patient.

The prime interest in the photo, though, is in the foreground, where a nurse, also masked/gowned/capped, also intense, holds an object toward both the viewer and the stainless steel receptacle about to receive it. In the nurse's gloved hands is a heart, resting gently, otherworldly still, its great vessels patulous and empty, turned eerily toward us. It is clearly the sick heart just removed from the chest of a patient now ready to receive a new transplanted one.

Mercy is everywhere in this photograph. Truth and Beauty are also present. Nevertheless, when one views a photograph of such terrible intensity, both the eye and the brain can be startled, even the conditioned, inured ones of the physician. The effect is so vivid that I feel as though I have witnessed, in the same instant, something truly priv-ileged, sacred, and horrific. The image in my mind's eye is somehow akin to that awe-filled moment when, after Salome's dance, John the Baptist's severed head was brought in on the silver tray. There is to me a curious rightness about that metaphor. For if this scene is incontrovertible proof of one death, it is also an adumbration of a life to come, one that will be richer and fuller for all the pain that went before.

But it is the invisible patient I want to keep in mind— the one who is, for the moment, heart-less, the heart-nest empty; the spirit asleep, oblivious, curled in the blessed arms of Morpheus and under the technologically skilled gaze of the whole transplant team, especially that of the anesthesiologist. For none of this life-giving, ethically laden, graceful surgery would be possible were it not for ether, that quintessential forefather of anesthetic mercy.

There has been, as it happens, no little controversy concerning the use of ether as an anesthetic agent. Its first administration is now generally attributed to Dr. Crawford W. Long, who utilized it in 1842 in a small Georgia town. Disputes having to do with historical priority have resulted in some well-known medical landmarks. They include the "Ether Dome" at the Massachusetts General Hospital in Boston and the Crawford W. Long Hospital of Emory University in Atlanta (as well as many other statues and memorials to Long and to others around the country).

The great ether controversy began when Dr. Crawford Long first used the substance to remove, painlessly, a tumor from the neck of one James Venable, in 1842. Subsequently, as pointed out by the historian Dr. Harvey Young in his 1983 address to the Anesthesia History Association, "Dr. Long used ether at least six more times before he read of the famous event, starring William T. G. Morton as anesthesiologist and John Collins Warren as surgeon, in the amphitheater of the Massachusetts General Hospital on October 16, 1846." The Boston event was promptly written up and appeared in the medical literature. But it was seven years after his first use of ether before Dr. Long, a busy country practitioner, finally got around to reporting his achievement. Long's supporters might laud his caution, suggesting that Long was attempting to be as certain as he could that the new drug was indeed the miracle that it seemed to be. Nevertheless, that Long was dilatory and, to use his own word, "negligent" in failing to report his use of ether sooner, is a judgment that cannot be denied. Long's detractors over the years have stressed, as Young points out, "the legitimate point that [Long] had failed in timely fashion to undertake the scientific obligation of presenting the evidence of his discovery." But the historical evidence for Long's priority in the first administration of ether as an anesthetic agent is otherwise unassailable.

None of this issue of precedence, historically important though it be, matters one soporific whit (or whiff) to the patient. What the patient wants is anesthesia, merciful, safe, and certain when it's needed. The word *anesthesia* is pure Greek: *an* (without) plus *aisthesis* (feeling). I have a personal interest in the etymology of this particular word. Ether wasn't used in my case, but one of its miraculous successors was. Twenty years ago, my right kidney had swollen up, hydronephrotic as a Georgia watermelon, because of a kidney stone lodged just above the ureter's entrance to the bladder. A urologist skilled in the use of what was ominously called a "basket" went after it and got it. Pre-op, all I recall is the anesthesiologist saying, "Dr. Stone, you may taste something like onion in your mouth." Then I slept, I forgot; as John Keats might have said, I was off to Lethe. In those minutes, mercy became personalized. It is true that when I woke up, easily, without nausea, and was helped up to urinate, it appeared that the entire and multitudinous Red Sea had filtered its incarnadine way down to my bladder. But—and this is the point—I had no pain during the surgery and was cured. There may be historical debates about attributions and priorities in anesthesia and its development, but, from the patient's point of view, there is no quarrel. What matters to the patient is mercy.

> *"Where Science touches man, it turns to Art."*
> —*John Ciardi*

Physicians are often told today, by voices both varied and insistent, that medicine is no longer the art it formerly was: technology has taken over. I disagree. The *possibility* of bringing into play the "art of medicine" in our encounters with patients has clearly been enhanced by today's technology. In that sense, and for the sake of honesty, I'd modify slightly the Ciardi quote: "Where Science touches man, *it has the possibility of turning* to Art."

Certainly, the possibilities for mercy in the practice of medicine have never been greater. The CAT scan, lithotripsy, magnetic resonance imaging, the echocardiogram, visual probes of all kinds, allow us to approach the patient in ways that were unimagined ten years ago. Such noninvasive advances embody their own forms of mercy. But nowhere is the possibility for mercy greater than in anesthesia, which has come so far, so fast, whether the surgery is for heart transplantation or a kidney stone. Perhaps old young John Keats, witness to only the crudest kind of anesthesia during his training, anticipates a more merciful time in his "Ode to a Nightingale":

> "Was it a vision, or a waking dream?
> Fled is that music:—Do I wake or sleep?"

Chest Pains:
What They Mean

"Be thou a spirit of health or goblin damn'd,
 Bring with thee airs from heaven or blasts from hell,
 Be thy intents wicked or charitable . . ."

—Shakespeare, *Hamlet*

$\mathcal{T}$he patient is an athletic, muscular policeman, thirty-one years old, with chest pain—a "heaviness" along his breastbone that has bothered him all day. As we talk I find that he has no risk factors for coronary disease; nor has he ever had pain like this before. After a while, he volunteers, a bit hesitantly, some additional and valuable information: Yesterday, on a challenge from his sergeant, he tried weight lifting for the first time. He did some bench presses (lifting weights while lying on his back) and was able to muscle up more than two hundred pounds! Then, this morning, the chest pain. I examine him, pressing my fingers along the sides of his breastbone, an inch or two from the center. He winces. Importantly, the pain is like that he has been having all day. When I tell him his pain is not coming from his heart, he exhales with a big whoosh, as if he had been holding his breath all day, and he smiles with great relief.

It seems to me that both physicians and patients view the heart with a certain ambivalence, a mix of feelings made up of approximately equal parts of respect and fear: respect because of the heart's ceaseless work; fear because of the perceived capriciousness with which heart disease may strike, with devastating consequences. Thus, pain in the abdomen may frighten us, but pain in the chest has the capacity to terrify, as though there could be something amiss in the very motor of life itself—and sometimes there just might be.

It's the physician's duty to sort out the myriad causes of

chest pain, which may arise not only from the heart but also from the lungs, esophagus, aorta and other vessels, from the bellows of the rib cage, even the abdomen. Some are benign; some are not. Newer technology, such as scans of the heart and lungs, have made the sorting-out easier. Chest pain as a diagnostic entity has so many variables that its analysis can be humbling to the best physician. Still, the starting point and often the most telling evidence is the patient's story. Let's begin with how a patient might describe angina.

Angina pectoris, literally "a strangling of the chest," is an old disease. In its typical form, it's not difficult to diagnose—William Heberden, the English physician who coined the term *angina pectoris*, did it in 1722: "They who are afflicted with it are seized while they are walking . . . with a painful and most disagreeable sensation in the breast, which seems as if it would extinguish life, if it were to increase or continue; but the moment they stand still, all this uneasiness vanishes." Angina, in its classical form, is usually brought on by exercise or emotional stress and relieved by rest. It's due to disease of the coronary arteries (cholesterol deposits or vessel spasm) that limits the amount of blood and oxygen available to the heart at times of increased demand. Patients often describe angina as a "heaviness" or "squeezing" in the center of the chest, behind the breastbone; the discomfort may radiate to the jaw or down one or both arms. (In some patients, pain occurs *only* in the jaw or arms, with no chest pain at all; still, in such cases, exercise or stress provokes the discomfort and rest relieves it.) Angina usually lasts one to five minutes (sometimes longer with emotional stress), subsiding as the cause is removed. Certain features may vary from patient to patient. For example, angina may be more likely to strike early in the morning, when the patient is rushing for work; the rest of the day may be pain-free. Walking into a cold wind or exercise after a meal provokes angina in some; in others, the emotional stress of a nightmare can do it. Exercise of the arm muscles—shoveling snow, say—may trigger angina in patients who never have an attack while walking (possibly because the larger leg muscles are more accustomed to heavy exercise). Angina is also known to be more common during the REM (rapid eye movement) portion of sleep, the stage that is associated with dreaming. This is understandable since, in some patients, emotional disturbance is more likely to cause angina than exercise alone.

A patient's medical history that is suggestive of angina may trigger a set of responses in the physician: a treadmill stress test, a thallium scan, or the "gold standard" angiography, in which dye is injected directly into the coronary arteries to examine the vessels. Efforts to find a simple and sensitive method of detection of coronary disease have resulted in the "stress-thallium" scan, which, unlike angiography, does not require catheterization. To perform this procedure, the physician injects thallium, a radioactive tracer chemical that goes through the bloodstream as the patient exercises on a treadmill. On the first pass through the heart, the thallium is avidly extracted by the heart muscle. The resulting distribution, seen on scanning equipment, helps locate the areas of arterial obstruction.

A last critical point: new onset angina or a changing anginal pattern (more frequent or prolonged pain) requires prompt evaluation. Either can warn of angina's serious cousin, a heart attack, in which heart muscle actually dies.

Certain *accompaniments* of chest pain may suggest that it is more serious. For example, any pain associated with shortness of breath, fainting or near-fainting, heavy sweating, weakness or exhaustion, or nausea deserves further assessment. This is also true for any chest pain severe enough to waken one from sleep.

Pleurisy deserves special mention. "Pleurisy" refers to sharp, lancinating chest pain made worse with each breath. Pleuritic pain suggests inflammation of the covering of the lungs (the pleura), which may occur, for example, in pneumonia. Inflammation of the lining of the pericardium, the sac that envelops the beating heart, may lead to similar pain.

Abdominal problems may masquerade as chest pain. Because nerves carrying impulses from the abdomen enter the spinal cord at about the same level as those from the heart, the gullible brain can be fooled into thinking that pain is *arising* from the heart, when it may in fact be coming from the esophagus, from an ulcer, or from the gallbladder. "Heartburn" from esophageal causes has, over the years, been a notorious mimic of angina.

But what of the many causes of pain that are *not* serious? The most common kind of chest pain, in all likelihood, is that caused by *anxiety* (which doesn't make it any less painful). In World War I, this association was recognized in soldiers on the front lines who were disabled by chest pain and shortness of breath. They received the mouthful diagnosis of "neurocirculatory asthenia," or simply, "soldier's heart." Such patients often complain of chest pain that is unrelated to exercise, located below the left nipple, either sharp and transient or dull and aching (I must avoid oversimplification: some patients with anxiety may have a prolonged aching under the breastbone that is difficult to distinguish from angina; and, of course, some patients with angina may have anxiety-caused discomfort as well. A thallium scan may help the clinician determine whether anxiety-induced pain is originating in the heart or is only a by-product of the anxiety.)

In some anxious patients, the full-blown "hyperventilation syndrome" is present—in addition to pain, patients with this disorder complain of difficulty in "getting in a good, deep breath" (though the problem is due to unconscious *over*breathing); they may also experience dizziness and tingling of the fingers and around the mouth. These symptoms are due to the overbreathing itself, which results in a lowering of the carbon dioxide level in the blood. Physicians may be tipped off to hyperventilation in a patient during the medical history: the patient heaves periodic deep sighs or yawns. My most memorable such case began on an airplane. A voice over the loudspeaker had asked whether there was a physician on board. I raised my hand, a bit reluctantly: one never knows what the problem might be, and it had been a number of years since I delivered a baby! But then the flight attendant escorted me to see a young man with chest pain. As he and I talked, I learned that not only was this his first flight, but that he was on his way to Parris Island, to marine boot camp! I did my best to reassure him. Then I applied the most effective, though unpretentious, first aid: I asked him to breath into a paper bag placed over his nose and mouth. His rebreathing of his own exhaled carbon dioxide restored his blood level to normal and led to a rapid "cure."

The "precordial stab" is another kind of innocent chest pain, one so common that almost everyone has experienced it at one time or another. Sudden, severe, knifelike, it's very short in duration, lasting only a second or two; it comes on when the patient is at rest—most often these days, while watching television in a slumped posture (the worse the program, the greater the slump). The stab of pain is usually in the left side, below the nipple (the "precordium," the area in front of the heart); this type of pain may also occur on the *right* side (but pain on the right side of the chest often goes unreported, since patients feel intuitively that such pain is not coming from the heart). Precordial stabs may cause the person to jump, or even cry out; then it recedes quickly with the next breath or with a change in posture. Possible causes include a cramp in the chest-wall muscles or a pinch of the chest wall nerves (which run along the undersides of the ribs). A similar kind of pain, called in children's and joggers' vernacular "a stitch in the side," may worsen with breathing and is most likely due to a cramp in the muscular diaphragm that divides the chest and abdomen.

What about our policeman-patient? The vulnerable anatomy of the chest wall can be blamed for his pain. The rib cage forms a kind of carapace for the chest. The ribs attach to the vertebrae in back, then sweep around the chest. In front, the last inch or so of rib, the part that attaches to the sternum, is not bone, but relatively soft cartilage. These rib–cartilage junctions are vulnerable to even minor injury, such as coughing might bring on (which explains the soreness along the sides of the breastbone in patients with the flu and severe coughing spells). With his bench presses, our policeman friend had strained every one of his rib–cartilage junctions; his outlook is, of course, very good.

When I was eighteen, a senior in high school, my father died of a heart attack. He died several days after the diagnosis was made, suddenly, unexpectedly, in the early morning. I remember well my last visit with him, the evening before; he smiled out at me through the plastic oxygen tent—coronary care units were off in the future. I think now that had he suffered the attack only ten years later, the technology of coronary care, new drugs, watchful and highly trained nurses, might well have saved him. Shortly after my father's death, I began to have chest pain. The physician who saw me—the same one who had attended my father—had the good sense to take a careful history, do an informed examination, and stop there. He told me that my pain was *not* from the heart, and suggested that I stop worrying about it. I did. I remember that moment clearly because it came like a gift.

There are many causes of chest pain, then, as I began to learn years ago. Some are serious; many are not. To know the difference is a step in the direction of bodily wisdom— and a good night's sleep.

Today, the fact that diagnosis and treatment for cardiac pain are infinitely better than they were a few decades ago is an excellent reason for concerned patients not to delay seeking help. For me, to be able to tell a patient (as is often the case) that his pain is *not* coming from the heart is one of the central joys of being a heart doctor.

Wearing of the Green

Many areas within the practice of medicine benefit from the "laying on of hands," preferably by a physician who makes generous use of his or her metaphorical heart. Of no specialty is this more true than oncologic/tumor surgery. As Dr. Francis Weld Peabody reminded us, decades ago, "One of the essential qualities of the clinician is interest in humanity, for the secret of the care of the patient is in caring for the patient." One such clinician is a colleague of mine; his practice also exemplifies Emily Dickinson's advice in the matter:

> "Surgeons must be very careful
> When they take the knife!
> Underneath their fine incisions
> Stirs the Culprit—*Life!*"

A friend and I are having an early lunch. She's an Aquarian; so, she tells me, am I. Out of curiosity, I ask her what the stars might say about someone born on November 15. She doesn't hesitate: "Scorpio," she says, ". . . and *tough*." November 15 is the birthday of Dr. Jack Coleman, whom I'm to meet at the operating room in an hour. His sign may be Scorpio—and there is a certain toughness about him—but his true sign is Cancer.

The sliding glass doors that lead to the surgical suite do not open as you approach them. In order to pass, you must press the small unobtrusive square on the wall nearby—the technologic equivalent of "Open Sesame." The doors swoosh and the smells of the operating room greet me: alcohol, anesthetics, clean cloth. In the dressing room, I pick out a "scrub suit," green cotton pants with a draw-string, a pullover top, cap, mask, shoe covers. I hang my clothes in Jack's locker, commit the locker combination to memory, and head for the OR.

The patient, fifty-five years old, with cancer of the tongue, is already asleep on the operating table. Three green-draped figures are clustered around him, surgeon, resident, nurse. (The three witches in *Macbeth* come to mind:

> "When shall we three meet again,
>   In thunder, lightning, or in rain?"
> "When the hurly-burly's done,
>   When the battle's lost and won.")

205

Surgery has already begun. First, tissue will be removed from the side of the neck—muscle and the lymph nodes along which the cancer could spread. Looking up briefly from his work, Jack Coleman greets me over his mask. For the delicate dissection, he's wearing spectacles to which are attached twin magnifying glasses, like jeweler's eyepieces. Just now, he's avoiding the nerves, the phrenic to the diaphragm, the vagus to the stomach, as they pass through the neck on their way to the lower parts of the body. The cancer, on the back third of the tongue, will then be removed. (The patient has already had radiation therapy to the area, in order to improve his chances.) Finally, a "skin flap" will be used to reconstruct the channel for swallowing. For the flap, skin over the upper arm will be moved to the surgical area, where its blood supply will be connected to neck vessels, using microsurgery. Microsurgery makes possible the connection of vessels no larger than the wire of a paper clip; such intricate feats require the use of an operating microscope, which is now being wheeled into position.

The microscope, six feet tall, angular and jointed, looks like a giant praying mantis, with an arm that moves up, down, and in a circle. Two eyepieces attach to the end of the arm. During surgery a sterile plastic wrap covers the eyepieces and barrel of the microscope. Foot pedals allow the surgeon to focus the microscope on the tissue being sutured, to "zoom" in and out, like a telephoto lens. A green plastic grid is placed, for contrast, under the tissue to be sutured. The optics of the system are exquisite: a five-millimeter (⅕-inch) section of the grid can be blown up until each millimeter looms like a ten-yard stripe on a football field. The thread used, nylon, is almost invisible, much finer than a human hair. The attached silver needle is also tiny, like a baby's curved eyelash. The operating microscope, vital for delicate eye operations, also makes possible the no-longer-rare reattachment of amputated extremities (including the penis). There is a printed warning

on the machine: READ INSTRUCTION MANUAL BEFORE YOU
OPERATE INSTRUMENT. A good idea—the machine costs
$60,000.

In our case, nine Lilliputian stitches are used to join the
ends of the vessels for the skin flap. The surgery is precise,
yet extensive, demanding and tedious: we are three-quarters
of the way through an eight-hour procedure. The patient
sleeps on, oblivious. "God, I'll bet he's going to be sore
tomorrow," I say from my vantage point, which looks over
a sterile sheet draped between the surgical field and the
anesthesiologist. "Nope," Jack says, "these patients have a
lot less pain then you'd expect—less than a gallbladder,
say." I stand corrected. The operation is going well. The
oxygen level in the patient's blood is being monitored
continuously; there is a steady hiss of anesthetic. Attention
to blood loss must be especially meticulous in this case: the
patient's religious beliefs (he is a Jehovah's Witness) preclude
his receiving a blood transfusion. (The students in my ethics
class may suspect at times that the faculty invents the cases
we discuss; the truth is, we couldn't concoct situations as
convoluted as those that face us daily.) Along the way, the
scrub nurse is spelled, but Dr. Coleman and the resident
work on through the dinner hour.

John Joseph Coleman, bred and born in Boston, is the
son of a shipyard foreman and a nurse. He went to private
school on a scholarship, made his way to Harvard College
and majored in Classics, Latin and Greek; then on to
Harvard Medical School before the computer matched him
to Atlanta and Emory for internship. He knew he wanted to
be a surgeon, but not precisely what kind. It took eight
more years after medical school for him to become an
oncologic (cancer) surgeon: five years of general surgery,
two years of plastic surgery, and one year of training in
cancer surgery.

"There has always been surgery for cancer, of course,
most of it done by general surgeons," Jack explains, leaning
back in his office chair. In his early forties, he has curly hair

and a gentle, slightly rounded face that reminds me a bit of the young Dylan Thomas, in the portrait by Augustus John. He continues, "As the field got more complex, some specialization developed."

Dr. Coleman has a special interest in cancer of the head and neck region: operations in this area are likely to require *all* of the knowledge he gained during his training, including his plastic and "reconstructive" surgery experience (which is helpful in minimizing some of the unavoidable postoperative cosmetic defects). There is an air of quiet self-confidence about Jack Coleman that reassures his patients, whatever their problem. Self-reliance is a quality shared by many good surgeons, including cardiovascular surgeons, the ones that I deal with most often. As in other difficult human endeavors, it's important for the cancer surgeon to face each morning with the attitude that no one else in the world can do this *particular* surgical procedure better than he (or she) can. Without that attitude, I suspect it would be better for the surgeon simply to roll over in bed and go back to sleep.

Cancer surgery *is* more complex now than before. At this week's tumor conference, a patient with medullary cancer of the thyroid gland was discussed. His disease was heralded not by neck problems, but by severe diarrhea caused by calcitonin, a substance secreted by the cancer. After surgery, the man's blood calcitonin levels will be monitored for recurrence of the tumor. Moreover, the patient's *relatives* will now be screened for this substance, which can serve as a biochemical "marker"; some relatives may need *prophylactic* removal of the thyroid to prevent a full-blown cancer and increase the cure rate. The days of the cancer surgeon as pure technician are over (if they ever existed); today's version must be mindful always of such biochemical warnings.

The day after the surgery, Jack and I see some patients together in the clinic. Our first is a heavyset fellow who can't talk: he had a laryngectomy for cancer fourteen years ago. As we enter he shakes hands with us and, moving his lips and mouth, makes breathy noises of greeting. "How're ya doin?" Jack asks. "Okay, I guess," the man replies in a rush of air. Jack fills me in on his history: "Mr. Ellis had his larynx removed in Tennessee. I saw him first three years ago, when the cancer recurred. Before that second surgery, Mr. Ellis had good 'esophageal speech,' could be understood over the phone, and so on. But since the surgery, his speech has been poor and that has bothered him a lot. He can't write, so speaking is his only way to communicate." Jack proceeds with his exam. "Mr. Ellis and I have been thinking together about an operation to place a prosthesis, a Blom–Singer 'artificial larynx.' You feel like you're ready for that now, Mr. Ellis?" The patient looks across the room to his son and they both nod. As we finish, they're shown around to the secretary to arrange for hospitalization.

The second patient is a woman who had a cancer, just below the lower lip, removed two years ago at another hospital. As the scar healed, the lip was "drawn down" in the process. When the cancer recurred six months ago, Jack operated. "The original incision was horizontal, here," he points out. "When I operated, I converted that first scar to a vertical one and the lip's not drooping anymore." I can tell that he—and she—are proud of the cosmetic, not to mention the medical, result. The scar would be completely invisible with a little makeup; in fact, we take a picture of her face so as to have a "before" and "after" for teaching purposes. The woman smiles broadly into the camera. She notes, looking especially toward the female resident with us, "Now when I put on lipstick, I can roll *both* my lips around." She shows us how. Some would see this as a small victory, but for her and the surgeon, it's a major one. Jack says he'd like to see her in three months. As he turns to leave, the woman says wistfully, "You don't ever make house calls, do you? I live only twenty minutes from Disney World." Jack promises to give her a call if he finds himself in that part of Florida. The contrast between her southern drawl and his residual Boston brogue is striking.

The sixty-year-old woman in the next room had cancer of the nasopharynx (deep in the nose area) three years ago. The tumor was not treated surgically, but with radiation. As a side effect of the X rays (her salivary glands were affected), her mouth is very dry, her sense of taste diminished. "I just eat to stay alive," she says, noting for us that she's lost thirty or forty pounds over the years. "But I *am* alive!" she says. Jack has begun his exam. Using a small round mirror and a head lamp, he eases her tongue forward and peers over the back of it. The visual effect is comparable to looking over the edge of a cliff. Far down, one can see the thin white *V* of the vocal cords opening and closing as she says a high-pitched "Eeee." She's very good at *not* coughing. (Years ago, when I was in medical school, I was selected as a "volunteer" on whom the professor could demonstrate to the class how such an examination should be done. I warned him: "I have a terrible gag reflex." "No problem," the professor said, "we'll spray the back of your throat." He did spray my throat, but I still almost coughed him out of the room.) Jack finishes his examination and has good news: "Everything's fine, Mrs. Johnson. Let's see you in six months.

The clinic continues, many patients take a long time, some are difficult cases, some easy, some triumphs. Jack moves from room to room, pressing the flesh, not superficially, as the politician presses, but deeply, down to the quick of things. The music of the afternoon is both dissonant and sweet, like the Bartók on my car radio as I head back to my office.

Two days after the tongue cancer surgery, Jack and I meet in the hospital coffee shop for a chat. The man is doing well, already up and around in his room. I've wanted a chance to ask Jack how he manages, emotionally, to deal with cancer patients day after week after year. Does it require a temperament different from that of other kinds of surgeons? "The older cancer surgeons used to tell me," Jack muses, "'Ya gotta *hate* cancer.' For a long time I thought that was a bunch of bull, but it's true. You *do* have to hate cancer. The operations are long and tedious and you sometimes have to deform the patient in order to help. But people get over operations pretty quickly; and, along the way, you develop this incredible bond with them." I remind Jack what William Carlos Williams, the poet-physician, wrote about the natural human desire for a cure: "We want *home runs,* antibiotics to cure man with a single shot in the buttocks." What, then, I ask, about the losses, the outright defeats, that occur in the life of a cancer surgeon? Jack replies, "Of course, there are home runs—and we savor them. But also, there is almost *never* someone that you can't help in *some* way." That statement, it seems to me, is the credo of a mature clinician, whatever his specialty: appropriately aggressive, realistic, compassionate. Even when time and the conspiracies of tissue align themselves against him and a given patient, Jack Coleman realizes that a *single*—a *bunt,* even—is still a commendable performance. It is a game plan a cardiologist can appreciate, a strategy that any major-league manager would applaud, whether the inning is early or late.

About the Author

John Stone is a physician who sees patients and teaches at Emory University School of Medicine. A cardiologist by training, he is also a poet whose three books are published by Louisiana State University Press. His essays have appeared frequently in *The New York Times Magazine*, as well as in *Discover, Massachusetts Medicine, MD Magazine, Memories,* and others. His writing has won a number of awards, including the award in literature from the Mississippi Institute of Arts and Letters. He has spoken and read from his work in well over half the fifty states.